W9-BLB-789

THE COLLEGE STUDENT'S

RESUME GUIDE

WRITING YOUR OWN

PROFESSIONAL RESUME

By Kim Marino

Tangerine Press

Ft. Collins, Colorado

Second Edition Copyright © 1991 by Kim Marino
First Edition Copyright © 1989 by Kim Marino
Printed in the United States of America
5 6 7 8 9 __ 92 91 90 89

All rights reserved including the right of reproduction or storage in whole or in part in any form, including photocopying without written permission from the author except for the inclusion of brief quotations in a review.

Names, addresses and phone numbers on all the resumes in this book have been changed to protect the privacy of each client.

Published by:

Tangerine Press
1315 Whedbee Street
Ft. Collins, CO 80524
U S A

ISBN 0-9624284-7-7

Cover Design by George Delmerico
Illustrations by Rod Tryon
Edited by Martin Perlman

ATTENTION: SCHOOLS, ORGANIZATIONS and CORPORATIONS
Quantity discounts are available on bulk purchases used for education, business or sales premium use. For information, please contact our Special Sales Department, Tangerine Press, (303) 224-5065, FAX (303) 224-4778 or write 1315 Whedbee Street, Ft. Collins, CO 80524.

INTRODUCTION

We seem to live in the age of the resume. You can study hard in school for four years, graduate with honors, and yet when it comes to getting that job, the first thing the interviewer asks of you is "a copy of your resume."

Yes, a resume, a good resume, is an essential part of your job search technique. A resume that works will represent you - your skills and accomplishments, leading the way for you to move from college into the work world.

Resume writing is an art in itself. I didn't have a guide such as this one to help me when I wrote my own first resume. In fact, if I only knew then what I know today, I could have saved myself lots of time and money. Actually, it took me years of writing professional resumes for students and professionals of all careers to perfect my resume writing skills. Now, however, I know what works and what doesn't. My method effectively creates resumes that capture each individual's most valuable assets.

Many of my student clients come to me frustrated; they had already been to resume writing seminars on campus, only to get more confused. Yet they realized the essential importance of a resume. And by the time we had finished creating the resume, you could see the excitement in their faces as they saw the final result. You, too, can learn my technique and put it to use simply by applying what you learn from this book...

After reading this text and using my principles, you'll have the ability to write your entire resume focused on your career objectives, a resume designed to get that interview!

Now in *The College Student's Resume Guide*, I've included everything you'll need to know to write your own professional resume. I'm confident you'll find this book one of the wisest investments you'll ever make.

ABOUT THE AUTHOR

Kim Marino is founder of Just Resumes™ in Santa Barbara, California and author of three nationally selling books *Just Resumes™, 200 Powerful and Proven Successful Resumes to Get that job,* published by John Wiley and Sons; *The Resume Guide For Women of the '90s* and *The College Student's Resume Guide*. She received her practical experience by being out there in the field, going on interviews and finding out what's going on in the business world. She learned what the employer is really looking for in a potential employee, essentially, what it takes to get an interview and what impresses the employer in the interview.

After spending 20 years working for other employers including 3 years researching the resume market and perfecting her writing style, Kim started a resume writing service. Personnel agencies, career counselors and a diverse range of clients quickly recognized her work; her referrals now extend throughout the nation and include men and women, professionals in dozens of fields, prominent members of business, industry and government as well as hundreds of college students. Scores of people have written to Kim thanking her for the resumes that have demonstratively improved their lives, and her resume writing service has become known as the #1 resume writing service to hundreds of satisfied customers.

ACKNOWLEDGEMENT

I would like to give special thanks to the following people for offering personal advice, opinions and aid in helping me put this book together:

George Delmerico the artist who designed the book cover. Rod Tryon, the artist who illustrated the artwork throughout the book. Steve Whitsett, the photographer who took my picture for the back cover. Publishers John and Susan Daniel and Dan Pointer for giving me the advice I needed to get this book published. Joe Marsh at the Earthling Bookstore for offering his book knowledge and expertise. Helen and Harry Kent for believing in me enough to help me get this book printed. Martin Perlman, freelance writer and former Senior Editor at *The Santa Barbara Independent*, for giving me the idea to write this book, for editing the manuscript and for moral support. This book was printed by McNaughton & Gunn, Saline, Michigan.

TABLE OF CONTENTS

INTRODUCTION

ABOUT THE AUTHOR

CHAPTER   **PAGE**

TABLE OF CONTENTS

TABLE OF CONTENTS

TABLE OF CONTENTS

CHAPTER   **PAGE**

Chapter I

WHAT IS A PROFESSIONAL RESUME?

Before Getting Started

To effectively use this book, first read all the text in Chapters I-IV. Then, review the resume samples to obtain an overall picture in your mind of what your resume will look like. You'll use the combination of text, scenarios and samples to guide you. Think about your background and what career you want to focus on. This will determine which format is best suited for you. Your choices are either functional, which focuses on your skills, or chronological, which emphasizes your jobs. You'll want to capture your strongest qualities. After you've finished your first draft, read your resume; then, review the text, scenarios and samples again as your reference guides to polish up what you've written.

What a Professional Resume Can Do For You

Your resume is a custom designed, self-marketing tool tailored to your career objectives. It's the first impression between you and the potential employer. A professional resume:

1. Focuses the interviewer's attention on <u>your</u> strongest points!
2. Gives you full credit for all your achievements, whether you got paid or not!
3. Guides the interviewer toward positive things to talk about in <u>you</u>!
4. Most importantly, it lets <u>you</u> see yourself in a more focused and positive manner!

Important Things to Know About the Resume

Resumes should be designed so that the receptionist involved in the resume screening process can look at the resume in a 30-second glance and decide to put it in the "Yes" pile. That's the pile that gets reviewed by the interviewer. A resume works most effectively in one or two pages; one page is best, if possible. It's very important to have an objective on your resume, even a general objective. The receptionist screening resumes does not want to take the time to figure out what position you're interested in applying for at the company. Also, you'll look more focused, and in turn, be more desirable for the position. As a rule, personal data does not belong on resumes (age, religion, shoe size, etc.). Personnel agencies tell me they've run across too much prejudice from the person screening the resumes (the receptionist in many cases), and the interviewer may never even see your resume.

The two basic types of resume formats are **functional** and **chronological**. Functional highlights your skills; chronological emphasizes your job positions. (We'll go into more detail on the differences between chronological and functional in Chapters II and III.) Most people are familiar with the chronological format, your traditional resume format. The functional and chronological resume should both offer the same basic information. The difference is only in how the information is presented.

The chronological resume is used when all these three points apply:
1. Your entire work history includes skills related to your objective.
2. Each position involves a completely different job description.
3. Your work history is stable. This is not as important now as it will be five years after you've graduated college.

The advantages of a functional resume format are stated below.
1. If your entire work history does not include skills related to your career objective, you'll create subsections, highlighting only those skills pertinent to your objective.
2. If you've had several positions with the same job description, you'll only say what you did one time, which saves the reader from having to read it over and over again. (See resume samples, Chapters IV and V.)

Why Is the Objective So Important on a Resume?

Here's a true story. A client phoned me one day and said she had had a resume professionally written for her by another resume writer. She was getting responses but for the wrong type of job. I discovered that her objective was in a cover letter and not in her resume. She was well qualified for several types of jobs but was only interested in one. Rewriting her entire resume, I added a job objective and designed a functional resume for her, adding subtitles directly related to her objective. In turn, the entire resume focused on her objective and she did get a response from the same company she'd written to before, this time for the position she wanted.

About Two-Page Resumes -- When They <u>Do</u> Work Best

While most students only require a one-page resume to get the job done, some of you may have an abundance of related experience requiring a two-page resume. Don't worry about it. You're better off having a well-written and properly formatted two-page resume than a poorly written or badly formatted one-page resume. So many students are terrified at the idea of having a two-page resume, they use smaller typefaces and cram too much information onto one page. NEVER DO THIS. These resumes will limit your chance to get interviews. No employer wants to bother with a resume that is too difficult to read.

Here's a couple of pointers for those of you with a two-page resume.

> ☞ Add - More - or - Continued - at the bottom of the first page.
> ☞ Place your name and page two at the top of the second page.

How to Determine What Typeface to Use For the Resume

Typeface is as important as the format you use for your resume. There are so many typefaces to choose from it can be mindboggling. Well, put your mind at ease. What you need is something that looks professional and is easy to read. The typeface should enhance your resume presentation, not dominate it. (See sample resumes in Chapters IV and V.) Avoid fancy script styles; opt instead for typefaces such as Helvetica, Century, Schoolbook or Times all available through Laser printing while using Desktop Publishing on the Macintosh or IBM computer system.

Selecting Good Quality Resume Paper

Color and texture are the important factors in selecting resume paper. For color, I highly recommend a conservative look for the business world. A brilliant white, ivory or light grey works quite well. For the technical fields, such as engineering or electronics go with the light grey. The brilliant white is suitable for the medical profession. Ivory works well for every profession.

If your field of interest is in the arts, such as a graphic artist, photographer or actress, you can be more daring and creative and use a blue or mauve color. Keep in mind in the arts you will also be submitting a portfolio of your work and may want to use it to show your creativity while sticking to a more conservative look for your resume. Personal preference plays a part in this too.

Always use a light colored, textured paper for your resume. There are many different textured papers for you to choose from. Parchment paper, for example, has a light textured background woven into the paper. Classic Laid, which also works great with resumes, has a heavier smooth wood-like finished look. Classic Linen has a lighter cloth-like textured look, and cotton, the most expensive, feels and looks just like cotton.

As with the typeface you choose, the resume paper should compliment your resume, not dominate it. Resume paper and matching envelopes are available at your local copy shop.

Chapter II
FUNCTIONAL VERSUS CHRONOLOGICAL

When to Use What

There are several different chronological and functional formats. What do they all have in common?

They all have the same basic titles:

- Name, campus and permanent addresses and phone numbers
- Career objective
- Professional profile
- Educational information
- Description of experience
- Honors and/or activities
- Employment history stating dates of employment, job title and company name, city and state

And please note:

- ☞ All sentences start with the appropriate action verb.
- ☞ They all focus on the career objective.

WHAT'S THE DIFFERENCE BETWEEN THE
STANDARD CHRONOLOGICAL & FUNCTIONAL RESUME?

- In the standard chronological resume, the experience and employment history is combined with dates of employment, job title, company name, city and state with description of experience listed in chronological order starting with the most recent and working backwards.

WHEN DO YOU USE A CHRONOLOGICAL RESUME?

- When your entire work history shows progress with skills directly related to your job objective.

- When each position involves a completely different job description.

- When you have a stable work history. (This is not as important as it will be five years after graduation.)

OR...

- If you've already had 1-3 internships, volunteer work or jobs directly related to your objective.

- Each position involves a completely different job description.

- And, you also have many unrelated jobs that you'd like to mention but they really are unrelated to your current objective.

WHAT MAKES THE FUNCTIONAL RESUME DIFFERENT FROM THE CHRONOLOGICAL RESUME?

- In the functional resume, all the work experience is highlighted with subsections created, pertinent to the job objective.

- The entire employment history is listed at the bottom of the resume with job title, company name, city and state in chronological order, separate from experience.

WHEN DO YOU USE THE FUNCTIONAL RESUME?

- When your entire work history goes beyond the skills and experience related to your objective.

- When you've had several positions with the same job description.

Chapter III
WRITING TECHNIQUES MADE SIMPLE

Effective Writing Techniques

In a professional resume a lot can be said concisely and vigorously. One-liners are simple, straightforward and work well for resumes. If you prefer paragraph form, that's fine too, though I like one-liners. Start each sentence with an action word, such as "assisted" or "organized," describing what you do. (See List of Action Words at the end of this lesson.) It's best not to use the same action word twice within a subsection or job description. Remember, for a functional resume, you will create a subsection. The title of each subsection will depend on what skills you highlight to focus on your career objective. (See resume samples, Chapters IV and V.)

> REMEMBER, ALWAYS THINK POSITIVE AND FOCUS
> ON YOUR JOB OBJECTIVE

Basic Questions to Ask Yourself For a Functional Resume

Remember the advantages of a <u>functional</u> resume format as listed below.

If your entire work history does not include skills related to your career objective, you'll highlight only those skills pertinent to your objective. A functional resume is selective.

If you've had several positions with the same job description, you'll only say what you did one time, which saves the reader from having to read the same material repeatedly. (See resume samples, Chapters IV and V.) A functional resume can convey a great deal of information in a minimum amount of space. Now, follow these instructions:

1. List your NAME

    How do you want your name to read on your resume?

2. ADDRESSES & PHONE NUMBERS

What are your permanent and campus addresses and phone numbers?

3. OBJECTIVE

What is your current objective? For example: a part-time position leading to a career in the film industry.

4. PROFILE

This is optional. Your profile is a brief description or summary of personal strengths, traits, and achievements related to the objective that the employer may be looking for in you. What are personality traits?

FOR EXAMPLE: Ability to comfortably work under highly pressured situations and consistently meet strict deadline schedules. (See resume samples chapters IV & V.)

5. EDUCATION

What's your major? Degree title? What school, graduating date?

Is your GPA above 3.0? If so, include it in the resume.

6. RELATED CLASSES

List 4-8 classes you've taken related to your objective. If you've had several years work experience, you don't need to include this information.

7. EXPERIENCE OR RELATED EXPERIENCE

What did you do at your job, paid or not? If you have no work history, that's okay; simply write about...

a. School projects you've worked on, related to your objective, or

b. Committees you've been on, or

c. Volunteer work you've done either on or off campus.

Remember to include any special achievements, directly related to your career objective. Always focus on your strongest points, directly related to your career objective. Look at resume samples and read scenarios for more details.

8.   HONORS/ACTIVITIES

List your title and date of honors and title, who you were actively involved with and date of your activities in this section.

FOR EXAMPLE: Dean's Honor List, 1989-90

Treasurer, Chi Omega Sorority, 1987-90

President, Rowing Club, Spring 1990

9.   EMPLOYMENT HISTORY

In this section, list your job title, company name, city, state and date position started/ended in chronological order, starting with the most recent and working backwards. If your job title is nondescript or if you didn't have a job title, that's okay. Simply use a title that describes what you did. Be consistent and list them in chronological order along with the other positions.

How to Organize the Raw Data in a Functional Resume

You'll gain a better perspective on what you're going to write about by listing your EMPLOYMENT or WORK HISTORY before writing about your experience. What you write about under the EXPERIENCE heading will be a description of your achievements and what you've done, taken directly from the EMPLOYMENT or WORK HISTORY and/or ACTIVITIES section. Remember, always focus on your career or internship objective.

Brainstorm your ideas. There really is no limit to the categories you can create. Start with an action word describing your experiences. After you've listed your achievements and experiences directly related to your career objective, sort out what you wrote. Then, create the subtitles that fit your descriptions of your career or internship objective.

FOR EXAMPLE: Let's say you're the Social Chairperson for a sorority, and you'd like a public relations internship. Even though this is a voluntary, unpaid position, you've probably gained valuable communication and organizational skills.

Basically what you're doing is describing the communication and organizational skills you've learned while being the Social Chairperson. Once you've completed writing about your experiences, create two subtitle sections:

1. communication skills
2. organization skills.

When using the above method, list each experience under the appropriate subheading. Visualize the employer receiving your resume. What is he/she looking for in you? Remember, the purpose of this resume is to get you an interview. You only want to write your achievements and experience related to your career objective.

Basic Questions to Ask Yourself For a Chronological Resume

I've found two different chronological formats that work great for students, depending of course on the individual's background. First, we'll discuss the standard chronological format.

✓✓✓ DO ALL THESE THREE POINTS APPLY TO YOU?

---

1. Your entire employment history shows progress with skills related to your objective.
2. Each position involves a generally different job description.
3. Is your work history stable? This will become more important after you've been in the work world for several years.

These rules apply to your standard chronological resume format. Simply follow the instructions below.

1. List your NAME

    How do you want your NAME to read on your resume?

2. ADDRESS & PHONE

    What are your PERMANENT & CAMPUS ADDRESSES & PHONE NUMBERS?

3. OBJECTIVE

    What's your current objective?

    FOR EXAMPLE: A growth-oriented position leading to a career in the fashion industry.

4. PROFILE

    This is a brief description or summary of your skills, personality traits, and achievements related to the objective. What are personality traits?

    FOR EXAMPLE: Let's say you want to be an accountant. The interviewer will look for someone who is detail oriented with the ability to meet strict deadline schedules.

5. EDUCATION

    What's your major? Degree title? What school, graduating date?
    Is your GPA average above 3.0? If so, include it in the resume.

6. RELATED CLASSES

    What are some of the related classes you've taken? List 4-8 classes. If you've had several years work experience, you don't need to include this information.

7. EXPERIENCE OR RELATED EXPERIENCE

    What DATE did you start your present job? (year starting/ending.) What's the

COMPANY (NAME, CITY and STATE) you presently work for? What did you do at your job, paid or not? At the end of each job description, mention what you learned.

FOR EXAMPLE: Let's say you're a Stress Peer Advisor. You can say that you "Learned to remain calm and in control under highly sensitive situations."

If you have no work history, that's okay. Simply write about...

1. School projects you've worked on, related to your objective, or
2. Committees you've been on, or
3. Internship or volunteer positions you've held.

Include any special achievements you've accomplished, related to your objective. Always focus on your strongest points, directly related to your career objective. Look at resume samples and read scenarios for more details. Be consistent and repeat the above questions under experience for each position pertinent to your objective.

8. HONORS/ACTIVITIES

List any honors and/or activities related to your objective. Being a committee member of a sorority, fraternity or club in college almost always will demonstrate related skills such as organization and communication applicable to almost any profession.

FOR EXAMPLE: **Dean's Honor List,** UCSB, 1988-90

Founding Member, Chi Omega Sorority, 1988

Treasurer, Chi Omega Sorority, UCSB, 1988-90

Tutor, University Tutorial Assistance Program, 1988-90

The Combination: Another Great Resume Format...

There is a variation of the chronological and functional format, which is called the Combination resume. It highlights experience related to your objective in the chronological style and lists your other employment in the functional format. Use the Combination format if the following points apply to your background.

1. You've already had 1-3 internships, some volunteer work or jobs directly related to your objective.
2. Each position involves a completely different job description.
3. And, you also have many other jobs you'd like to actually mention, but they are unrelated to your current objective. (See resume samples in Chapter V, Thomas, Law & Society major and Karla, Political Science major.)

Simply follow the same instructions for the internships, volunteer work or jobs directly related to your objective listed under RELATED EXPERIENCE (see number 7, above). This time you will also create a section for your unrelated jobs titled EMPLOYMENT HISTORY and list them at the end of your resume. List your job title, company name, city, state and date position started/ended for the rest of your jobs in chronological order starting with the most recent and working backwards.

NOTE, if you've had several jobs over the years, it is unnecessary to list all of them. For example, if you've had five seasonal jobs in one year, you can select from among them. List the jobs (under the Employment History section) you don't need to go into detail about but which are worth mentioning to show you have been gainfully employed.

Resumes for the Arts

Those of you entering a profession in the arts, such as Photographer, Actress, Graphic Artist, or Actor, probably worked on related projects for school or freelance projects for friends, family or clients. If so, you'll want to call your work experience CLIENTS/PROJECTS. Simply list the name of the person, school or company the work was for and briefly describe your project.

For the artist, list your clients/projects this way:

CLIENTS/
PROJECTS: Kim's Boutique - Designed and illustrated six line art promotional posters.

If you're an actress or actor, under Theatrical Experience say this:

> <u>**Performing Experience**</u>
> <u>Lead-Marvin</u>, "March of the Falsettos," Boston University, Boston, MA.

Resume Do's and Don't's

- **DO** choose a job that you "love".

- **DO** spend time listing ALL your good qualities. This is where you get credit where credit's due.

- **DO** include a job objective, clearly and concisely and focus your resume on your future objective to show the employer "where I am going," not "where I have been or where I am now."

- **DO** include experience/skills directly related to job objective.

- **DO** start each sentence with an action word.

- **DO** list all related experience...paid or unpaid. Include experience from school activities and committees such as organizing fundraising events, sorority/fraternity treasurer or social chairperson, etc.

- **DO** research the position and company before the interview.

- **DO** keep your resume down to one or two pages.

- **DO** follow-up the interview with a personalized thank you letter.

- **DON'T** leave out the job objective.

- **DON'T** include material or history not related to the job objective.

- **DON'T** use long, repetitive explanations.

- **DON'T** include personal history.

- **DON'T** presume that the "personnel screener" understands skills included in job title--tailor your job description.

- **DON'T** take for granted skills that you perform well as a matter of course.

- **DON'T** replace a job description with a job title--it's not self-explanatory. A manager in one company may not do the same activities as a manager in another company.

- **DON'T** forget to include your GPA under education, if it's a 3.5 or higher.

- **DON'T** list references from whom you have not received permission or a positive response.

- **DON'T** send a "form" thank you letter. Personalize each one.

- **DON'T BE AFRAID TO SHOW OFF YOUR SKILLS!**

LIST OF ACTION WORDS

act as	effect	plan
active in	enact	prepare
administer	establish	present
allocate	evaluate	process
analyze	edit	produce
approve	execute	proofread
articulate	examine	promote
assimilate	follow-up	propose
assist	forecast	provide
assure	formulate	perform
augment	forward to	persuaded
balance	generate	recommend
built	guided	repaired
collect	identify	recruit
communicate	implement	report
compute	inform	research
conceptualize	initiate	resolve
consolidate	integrate	review
consult	interface	revise
contribute	install	represent
control	institute	referred
coordinate	interview	schedule
correct	instruct	screen
correspond	launch	secure
counsel	liaison	select
create	locate	set up
coach	lecture	supervise
chair	lead	supply
demonstrate	maintain	specify
design	manage	systematize
determine	monitor	stimulate
develop	mediate	summarize
direct	market	strengthen
distribute	optimize	test
document	organize	train
draft	oversee	tabulate
delegate	operate	upgrade

Chapter IV
RESUME SAMPLES & CASE HISTORIES

About Resume Samples and Case Histories

The following pages in this chapter consist of eight case history scenarios with resume samples for each client. Each scenario explains the background of the student who came to me for help in writing that all-important resume. The scenario explains which format works best and why. There is a brief explanation of the procedure used to write each resume, and you'll see the results in the accompanying sample. Read each one carefully. Then, think about your own background and how it applies to the job or internship you'll want to write your resume for.

REMEMBER, it's important that you read all the text in Chapters I-IV and review the resume samples in this book to give you a complete sense of what you need to write an effective resume.

Searching For the Right Career For You

If you're still not sure what you'd like to do, look through the want ads in your local newspaper. See what interests you. Another helpful idea is to combine your hobbies with your skills.

> **FOR EXAMPLE:** Let's say you like athletics and work well with people; maybe you'd like to consider working for a manufacturer of athletic clothing or equipment as a sales or marketing representative. Read Chapter VII, JOB SEARCHING AND INTERVIEWING for effective job search techniques used to find positions that aren't always advertised.

Another useful strategy is going to on-campus interviews, which will not only give you terrific interviewing experience but will also introduce you to many good companies. This is a great way of finding out what's really out there. I've had many college student customers who had no idea what they preferred to do until they went to several on- campus interviews. Some students thought they knew what they wanted but changed their minds after interviewing on campus with several potential employers.

And believe it or not, friends and family can be an excellent source of job opportunities. Many times someone knows someone who just mentioned to your best friend that there's an opening for the very kind of job you're interested in at a company in town. Or an uncle who works in the field you're entering may be able to recommend a certain manager or owner you could speak with.

CASE HISTORY: DENISE
Business Economics Soon to be Graduate Seeks Accounting Career

Denise is a student seeking an entry level accounting position after graduation.
In the Professional Profile, I detailed skills she has to offer based on the needs of an accounting firm.

Notice how I highlighted all her accounting skills and included her coursework at the end. Also, notice that every line starts with a different action word describing what she did.

The chronological resume works well for Denise. Her work history is stable and includes skills related to her profession, and each position involves a completely different job description.

DENISE A. LITTLE

Current Address	**Permanent Address**
4999 College Road	1111 Marina Avenue
Goleta, CA 93117	Concord, CA 94333
(805) 222-0800	(222) 888-8888

Objective: Entry Level position leading to a challenging Accounting career.

PROFESSIONAL PROFILE
- Highly organized, dedicated and committed to professionalism.
- Work well under pressure with attention to detail.
- Excellent written, oral, interpersonal communication skills.
- Active member of the Philanthropy Committee and Scholarship Committee.

ACCOUNTING SKILLS
Profit and loss statements...income statements...accounts payable ...payroll...bank reconciliation...general ledgers and journals... balance sheets...trial balance...strong computerized accounting. Coursework: Individual, Partnership & Corporate Tax Accounting... Intermediate Accounting...Micro & Macro Economic Theory...Auditing.

PROFESSIONAL EXPERIENCE
Bookkeeper/Data Entry, Gustin & Associates, San Francisco   1987-present
- Maintain computerized accounts for small businesses on the IBM PC computer.
  - Prepare income statements, bank reconciliation, general ledgers, journals, balance sheets and trial balance, meeting demanding deadline schedules.
  - Interface with clients to analyze business needs and maintain better records.
  - Enter data on IBM System 34 computer using a custom financial software program.

Personnel Assistant, Martin Corporation, San Francisco, CA   Summer 1988
- Assisted management with personnel recruitment and orientation meetings.
  - Involved answering phones, filing and accurate recordkeeping on a daily basis.

Customer Service Representative, San Francisco Chronicle, San Francisco, CA   1984-86
- Created solutions in the customer complaint department on a daily basis.
  - Developed phone skills, expediting challenges customers presented quickly and creatively.
  - Excellent problem solver, dealing with irate customers in a professional and diplomatic manner under highly pressured situations.

EDUCATION
BA Degree, Business Economics, June 1990
University of California at Berkeley
Accounting GPA: 3.8   Overall GPA: 3.6

CASE HISTORY: MARK
Architectural Design Major Seeks Part-time Related Work

Mark, my nephew, came to me one day and said, "There is no way I can find a job in an architectural firm because I'm only in my first year of college and I have no experience." Later, Mark called me from Arizona and asked me to help him. I interviewed him over the phone.

In the Professional Profile, I listed skills he has to offer based on the needs of an architectural firm. Since Mark is a student, I added a list of all related classes he's taken in school. I knew Mark had been working since he was in high school in unrelated jobs. But I also knew that those unrelated jobs had related qualities such as employee and customer relation skills helpful in getting a job in an architectural firm.

After talking to Mark, I learned that he worked on several architectural projects in high school as well as college. I created an appropriate subtitle under experience and asked him what projects he worked on. Architects need to have strong communication skills. Mark has developed these skills through his previous employment. So, I created the appropriate subtitles based on Mark's background, focused on his objective, and asked him to describe his customer and employee relation responsibilities. His job titles, company names, city, state and dates of employment are listed in chronological order. Again, all the basic information written in this functional resume is the same as a chronological resume. The only difference is the method of presentation, which changes the focus . . . allowing what Mark had done to surface. Mark didn't realize it when he first called me, but he is a perfect candidate for part-time employment at an architectural firm. The employer feels the first or second year architectural design students will stay with the firm at least until they complete college and get a degree. Mark now sees himself in a more focused and positive manner.

MARK STEVEN MARINA

Permanent Address
333 Jerry Ave
Los Angeles, CA 10001
(213) 555-1222

Campus Address
234 East Apache
Tempe, AZ 85222
(602) 921-2305

Objective: A part-time position leading to a career in Architecture

PROFESSIONAL PROFILE
- Four years experience in line drawing.
- Learn quickly, creative in conceptual architectural design.
- Lifetime interest; willing to learn all aspects of architecture.
- Communicate well with customers and professionals.
- Detail oriented, problem solver and team player.
- Take directions and follow through to completion.

EDUCATION
BS Degree Architectural Design, 1992
Arizona State University, Tempe, AZ

Related Classes: Freehand Drawing I&II
Design Graphics, Environmental Design, Arch. 5

RELATED EXPERIENCE
Residential Architectural Projects
- Designed a poolhouse on the CAD CAM system.
- Successfully developed conceptual design and drew the whole set of plans for a 2000 square foot beachhouse.
- Designed the development of a three-story townhouse.
- Created the conceptual design for a family room addition.

Customer & Employee Relations
- Assisted the owner of a company to set up an entirely new retail store.
  - Involved inventory control, shipping & receiving, pricing, setting up lighting fixtures, clothing racks and assembling furniture.
- Interfaced with customers interpreting their needs in a professional and courteous manner.
- Assisted employees simultaneously in all phases of a busy fast food restaurant. Maintained opening procedures and cash management.
- Developed excellent communication skills with employees and customers.

EMPLOYMENT HISTORY

Telecommunication Sales, Tempe America, Tempe, AZ	Spring 1989
Data Entry/Sales/Warehouse, Cousin's Children Store, LA, CA	1985-88
Cashier/Cook, In & Out Burger, Los Angeles, CA	1984-85

CASE HISTORY: PEGGY
Changing Careers to Real Estate Associate

Peggy is getting her real estate license and wants to become a real estate agent. She's never professionally worked with real estate before, but she did assist her husband in the design, construction and sale of their own condominium. So, I created a subheading under experience and asked her what she did to achieve this. It came across quite well in her resume.

Real Estate agents need to have strong communication and organizational skills. From being an instructor, Peggy has sales, promotions and client relation skills. That's why I developed the appropriate subtitles based on Peggy's background and focused on her objective. I then asked her to describe to me what her client relations, sales, promotion and organizational skills were. In the Professional Profile, I highlighted skills she has to offer based on the needs of a real estate agent. Since Peggy knows she specifically wants to be a real estate associate, I decided to highlight that in big bold letters, which becomes her objective.

Notice, under Employment History, I still have her job titles, company names, city, state and dates of employment listed in chronological order. Again, all the basic information written in this functional resume is the same as a chronological resume. The only difference is the way it's presented. Also, notice that every line starts with a different action word describing what she did. Once you begin writing in this style, it really becomes quite effective because it's consistent and works so well with resumes.

Peggy's background is a perfect example of where a functional resume works best to bring out skills and attributes she might never have thought to list.

PEGGY JUSTIN
111 Butter Lane
Santa Barbara, CA 93111
(805) 599-2345

REAL ESTATE ASSOCIATE

PROFESSIONAL PROFILE
- Outstanding talent for assessing people's needs.
- Proven ability to gain clients' confidence and trust.
- Gained valuable business and personal contacts throughout the Los Angeles and Ventura Tri-county areas.

RELATED EXPERIENCE

Real Estate Experience
- Assisted in the design, construction & sale of a Los Angeles condominium.
- Established an effective marketing strategy to promote the sale of property.
  - Designed flyers and newspaper advertising; distributed flyers.
  - Arranged and conducted open house.
- Familiar with blueprints and architectural plans; understand conceptual design.

Sales, Promotions & Organization
- Organized and coordinated an entire summer tennis program for children at a private tennis club in Montecito.
- Promoted services through effective telemarketing techniques, thorough product knowledge and exceptional client relations.
- Compiled computer data to keep track of profits & losses of monthly sales.

Client Relations
- Interface with clients and members to interpret their needs and priorities.
- Develop innovative, non-competitive teaching techniques for adults and children, focusing on individual strengths.
- Advise clients and members in a professional manner, securing trust and confidence.

LICENSE
California Real Estate Salesman's License, 1989

EMPLOYMENT HISTORY

Tennis Instructor, <u>A Tennis Club</u>, Montecito, CA	1987-present
Teacher's Assistant, <u>Los Angeles School District</u>	1985-87
Pre-School Teacher, <u>Children's Pre-School</u>, LA, CA	1983-85

CASE HISTORY: BRIAN
Geological Science Graduate Seeks Geologist Position

Brian's employment history is unrelated to his objective. His related experience is through school projects, so we wrote his resume in a functional format. We highlighted all his skills and experience directly related to his objective and listed in chronological order his employment history.

Again, it's a matter of emphasizing what is most important in relation to the job you're seeking. Brian was not only pleased by the way in which his earlier experiences were shown to lead directly to the position, he also gained a sharper perception of what he had been pursuing and why.

BRIAN B. MATTHEWS
118 Franciso Avenue
Ventura, CA 93003
(805) 966-7281

Objective: Entry level Professional Geologist position

EDUCATION:

BS Degree, Geological Sciences
University of California, Los Angeles
Graduation: June 1991

Geoscience Technology, Certified: 1987
Los Angeles City College, CA
Petroleum Geology emphasis

AS, Geological Sciences
Los Angeles City College, CA
Graduation: June 1986

HONORS:

- Top of class; six week summer field course, UCLA 1988
- Outstanding Geoscience Technology Major, LACC, 1986
- Selected for Honors Seminar, The Colorado Plateau, LACC, 1985

GEOLOGY SKILLS:

Petroleum geology, well logging, microfossil collection and analysis...electric log analysis, geophysics, methods in gravity, magnetics, resistivity, seismics, geologic illustration, geochemistry, ore mineralogy, structural geology.

Gained valuable field knowledge and experience. Mapped Paleozoic sedimentary, volcaniclastic rocks in Inyo and Alpine County and local formations of the Santa Ynez Mountains in Santa Barbara County, California. Mapped in Cuyama Badlands, Kern County, California.

Experienced on the IBM and Macintosh computer systems.

EMPLOYMENT HISTORY:

Carpenter, Blakely Construction, Goleta, CA	1987-present
Carpenter, Glen Construction, Goleta, CA	1983-87
Carpenter, McIntosh Construction, Mammoth Lakes, CA,	1980-83

CASE HISTORY: PAUL
Business Economics Graduate Seeks Corporate Accounting Position

Paul had worked at one company for the past four years. Notice how we highlighted his experience by adding subtitles that describe the important skills the interviewer will look for in an entry level corporate accounting position.

Also notice how we added an accounting skills category to highlight quickly his general accounting skills.

This is an excellent example of the many hidden job skills that lurk in your job history. A functional resume, allows you to give yourself full credit for your varied activities.

PAUL BLACK
999 College Avenue
Santa Barbara, CA 93105
(805) 555-1111

Objective: A Corporate Accounting position.

PROFESSIONAL PROFILE
- Highly organized, dedicated with a positive attitude.
- Work under strict deadline schedules with attention to detail.
- Financed education with experience in computerized accounting and management.

EDUCATION
BA Degree, Business Economics, 1991
University of California, Los Angeles

ACCOUNTING SKILLS
Profit and loss statement, balance sheet, trial balance, general ledger and supporting journals, accounts receivable, payroll, bank reconciliation, strong computerized accounting skills.

EXPERIENCE

STRUCTURAL ACCOUNTING SYSTEMS, Los Angeles, CA   1985-1991
Financial Statements & Computer Skills
- Prepared financial statements under cash and accrual accounting methods for sole proprietorships, partnerships, S and non-profit corporations.
- Converted manual accounting systems to a computerized accounting system for clients.
- Designed custom spreadsheet programs for internal use as well as for clients.

Billing, Payroll & Client Relations
- Prepared billing and maintained accounts receivable for private water companies and homeowners' associations.
  - Learned to interpret customer's needs efficiently; solve potential problems in a diplomatic & courteous manner, under sometimes sensitive situations.
- Generated payroll checks and reports.

Management & Organizational Skills
- Reported directly to the owner of the company.
- Assisted in establishing a successful structure for a growing company.
  - Trained and supervised employees, maintaining a professional manner.
  - Helped prioritized work schedules and delegated assignments.

CASE HISTORY: CHRISTOPHER
Law and Society Major Seeks Student Affairs Officer Position

Christopher is applying for a specific position as a Student Affairs Officer at a university. The Student Affairs Officer works directly with the Educational Opportunity Program (EOP) at this same university. Since Christopher went through this program himself and gained personal insight about the program, we decided to highlight the knowledge he learned from this hands-on experience.

Christopher has also developed and organized several programs and committees while in college. He represented his fraternity as well as other organizations and gained valuable public speaking skills needed for this position.

All the valuable skills Christopher gained pertinent to the Student Affairs Officer position are through volunteer work and personal experiences. These experiences make Christopher an outstanding candidate for this position.

CHRISTOPHER B. FRANCES

Current Address
22 Churchill Drive
Santa Barbara, CA 93110
(805) 555-1111

Permanent Address
225 Westwood Drive
Los Angeles, CA 90043
(213) 555-2345

Objective: Student Affairs Officer.

EDUCATION
BA Degree, Law and Society, June 1990
University of California, Los Angeles

RELATED EXPERIENCE

Educational Opportunity Program (EOP)
- A Student Affairs Officer from UCLA recruited me from Valley College to this program.
- Gained valuable knowledge and personal insight at UCLA through the experience of transferring to a 4-year university from a community college.
  - Became keenly aware of situations students face and look forward to the opportunity of passing this knowledge on to them. Such as...
  - counseling resources available to guide me through this program.
  - peer/faculty support network available to minority students who qualify to be admitted to UCLA; tutorial services made available.

Organization & Promotions
- Organized an effective alcohol and risk reduction program.
  - resulted in reduced financial liability for incidents involving the Greek community.
- Coordinator for GRACE, an awareness committee to increase minority involvement in the Greek community.
- Developed a support network organization of American Indian college students.
- As Alumni Committee Member, contacted members to promote fund raising events.
- As Rush Committee Member, created promotional themes for fraternity annual events.

Public Speaking Skills
- Represented fraternity to promote fund raising events for the American Cancer Society and Diabetic Association.
- Conducted meetings and presented ideas on the formation and structure of the Organization of North American Indian College Students.
- Prepared several speeches and conducted presentations and seminars.
- Learned to speak confidently and fluently in front of large groups.

EMPLOYMENT HISTORY

Resident Coordinator, University of California, LA, CA — 1988-89
Sales Assistant, Standard Brands, Los Angeles, CA — Summers 1985-87
Corporate Security Guard, Trans-America, Los Angeles, CA, — Summer 1984

CASE HISTORY: MARK
English Literature Major Seeks Marketing Internship

Mark has had extensive experience in communications, administration and organization while being president of the college English Club for two years. This is where Mark gained valuable skills pertinent to a marketing internship.

We focused his entire resume on these skills. This experience makes Mark an excellent candidate for a marketing internship.

You'd be surprised how many students make use of volunteer activities to gain an internship position. That internship position can then lead to full-time work in the profession of your choice. Nothing need go to waste in a professional resume!

MARK C ROMERO
75 College Ave
Goleta, CA 93117
(805) 555-1111

Objective: A Marketing Internship

PROFESSIONAL PROFILE
- Highly organized, dedicated with a positive attitude.
- Resourceful; skilled in analyzing and solving problems.
- Good written, oral and interpersonal communications.
- Team player with proven leadership qualities and ability to supervise with professionalism, diplomacy and tact.
- Work well under pressure situations with the ability to meet demanding deadline schedules.

RELATED EXPERIENCE

UNIVERSITY OF CALIFORNIA, Los Angeles   1987-90
English Club President

Administration & Organization
- Delegate work and supervise staff members.
- Write proposals and appear before the Finance Board to renew annual budgets.
- Coordinate academic, cultural and social activities.
- Conduct bi-weekly meetings; coordinate guest speakers and field trips.
- Maintain finances and accounting procedures including auditing and annual budget forecasting for student organization.

Communications
- Compose announcements, newsletters and correspondence focused on organizational activities for the campus community.
- Assist members with research projects on a daily basis.
- Respond quickly and efficiently to inquiries, solving problems for members in a professional and concerned manner.
- Recognized by the University of California for effective public speaking.

EDUCATION

BA Degree, English Literature
University of California, Los Angeles
Graduation: 1992   GPA: 3.7

CASE HISTORY: HOLLY
Sociology Major Seeks Sales/Management Trainee & Teacher Position

---

Since Holly is skilled for and wants to apply for two entirely different professions, we wrote one resume for each profession. See how focused she looks in each resume. The format is the same but each is entirely focused on her objective.

The chronological format works well for Holly because each position she held shows a different job description directly related to her objective. Also notice: In the sections "professional profile," "education," "related coursework" and "experience," each resume focuses all her skills directly related to each profession.

Holly's is not an uncommon situation. Many college students (and professionals) have had a number of jobs--that very variety can ultimately allow you to expand into new job opportunities.

HOLLY L. BLAKE

Current Address	**Permanent Address**
111 Camarillo #1	2215 Oak Street
Goleta, CA 93117	San Francisco, CA 94361
(805) 362-8899	(415) 888-1177

Objective: Grades K-6 Teaching position

PROFESSIONAL PROFILE:
- Team player with teachers, administrators and parents.
- Work well in a competitive and challenging environment.
- Skilled problem solver with proven leadership qualities.

EDUCATION:
- California Basic Educational Skills Test (CBEST) Passed in April 1989.
- **BA Degree, Sociology,** June 1990 University of California, Los Angeles

CLASSROOM EXPERIENCE:

1988-90 **PRE-PROFESSIONAL VOLUNTEER INSTRUCTOR**
El Camino Elementary School, Los Angeles School District
- Assisted teacher with instruction of 3rd grade students with daily classroom activities in all areas of the curriculum.
  - Worked with groups as well as on a one-on-one basis.
- Concerned with the total growth and needs of the child involving social, emotional, intellectual, creative and physical behavior.
- Built child's self-esteem and self confidence. Effectively motivated children to maximize participation and enjoyment.
- Supervised children on field trips.

Fall 1987 **PRE-PROFESSIONAL VOLUNTEER INSTRUCTOR**
Blakely School, Los Angeles School District
- Assisted the teacher with instruction of kindergarten children.
  - Worked with children on a one-on-one basis and in small groups in this classroom of 20 students.
- Identified and provided assistance to children needing special attention with above or below average skills.
  - Promoted behavior based on respect for others, teaching children to communicate their feelings and to hear each other.
  - Provided consistent behavior/progress, each child at their own pace.
  - Focused on respect for child's strengths & unique personality.
- Supervised art projects, math games and worked with children on manipulative math activities and reading readiness.

HOLLY L. BLAKE

Current Address
111 Camarillo #1
Goleta, CA 93117
(805) 362-8899

Permanent Address
2215 Oak Street
San Francisco, CA 94361
(415) 888-1177

Objective: A Sales/Management Trainee position

PROFESSIONAL PROFILE:
- Financed education with three years experience in sales and supervision in the retail, health fitness industries.
- Highly organized, dedicated with a positive attitude.
- Outstanding ability to communicate with all types of people.

EDUCATION:
BA Degree, Sociology
University of California, Los Angeles
Graduation: June 1988

EXPERIENCE:

Summer 1987   THE TENNIS CLUB, Los Angeles, CA
Club Supervisor
- Managed entire operations and hired, trained and supervised five employees in the cafe at this busy private health/fitness club.
- Provided assistance to members with professionalism, expediting challenges members presented in a quick and efficient manner.
- Maintained inventory and scheduling; met demanding deadlines.
- Required a positive attitude with superior customer relations.

Fall-86   UNIVERSITY OF CALIFORNIA, Los Angeles, CA
Telecommunication Representative
- Demonstrated effective cold calling and telemarketing techniques for the Annual Fund.
- Communicated with recent graduates and parents to generate funds and receive new donations for the Annual Fund.

1984-85   KATHY'S OFFICE SUPPLIES, Los Angeles, CA
Retail Sales
- Sold Hallmark products and office supplies through excellent sales ability and thorough product knowledge.
- Demonstrated excellent customer relation skills and built a large personal customer base.
- Designed in-house displays that promoted store sales.
- Maintained inventory, quality control opening/closing procedures, cash management.

Chapter V

ADDITIONAL RESUME SAMPLES

About the Additional Resume Samples

The following pages in this chapter consist of 16 more resume samples for college students of various majors focusing on their individual goals. You will see a variety of formats to choose from in functional and chronological styles. This chapter is divided into two sections.

- ▸ First is a variety of functional resume format samples.
- ▸ Second is a wide range of chronological resume format samples including the combination and artist resume style resume samples.

Look at each resume carefully. Again, think about how your own background applies to the job or internship you'd like to obtain.

REMEMBER, it's important that you've already read all the text in Chapters I-IV before reviewing the resume samples in this chapter. The "how-to" information in the first three chapters plus the samples in Chapter V will provide you with the necessary tools to write an effective resume.

STACIA ANN BURGANDY

6111 Frio, Goleta, CA 93117   (805) 888-4040

Objective: An Internship in Business and Finance.

PROFESSIONAL PROFILE
- Financed education with experience in sales, cash management and customer relations.
- Highly organized, enthusiastic with a positive attitude.
- Outstanding ability to communicate with all types of people.
- Member of Community Affairs; part of the Big Sister program.
- Secretary/Treasurer for the UCLA English Club.

PROFESSIONAL EXPERIENCE
Organization/Cash Management
- Set up/planned meeting agendas and prepared minutes for school activities.
- Balanced daily cash deposits with speed and efficiency for the college bookstore, grocery store and stationary retail store chain.
- Maintained opening and closing procedures, inventory/quality control, shipping/receiving, purchasing, pricing, returns and credits.

Sales Ability & Promotions
- Successfully sold Hallmark products and helped customers make satisfactory buying decisions at a busy retail store.
- Sold books and accessories at the college bookstore.
- Set up in-house displays that instantly boosted sales.

Customer & Employee Relations
- Developed a personal customer base while waiting tables at a busy family style restaurant.
  - Required ability to work well under pressure situations quickly and efficiently.
- Demonstrated strong phone skills, expediting challenges customers presented in a professional and concerned manner.
- Trained and supervised 6 employees, maintaining excellent staff relations.

EDUCATION
BA Degree, Business Economics, Spring 1989
University of California, Los Angeles

EMPLOYMENT HISTORY
Waitress/Cashier, Baker's Square Restaurant, LA, CA   1987-present
Cashier/Sales, University of California Bookstore, LA, CA   1986-1987

CYNTHIA A. FRANCHESCA
222 Tool Street
Santa Barbara, CA 93101
(805) 222-8080

Objective: A position in Marine Biology

PROFESSIONAL PROFILE
- Highly organized, dedicated with a positive attitude.
- Ability to handle multiple assignments in highly pressured situations and consistently meet tight deadline schedules.
- Excellent written, oral and interpersonal communication skills.
- Thrive on working in a challenging work environment.

EDUCATION
BS Degree, Marine Biology, 1992
Northridge State University, Northridge, CA

Washington Institute of Marine Biology
University of Washington, Seattle, WA
Summers 1980-81

EXPERIENCE

Organization/Coordination
- Coordinated and wrote marine biology research projects.
- Designed a study of kelp flies in a marine biology research project; located species and measured quantity.
- Photographed coverage through a microscope of an animal behavior study.
- Organized projects for an aviation company working closely with engineers and customers; involved blueprints, correspondence and manual updates.

Marine Biology Experience
- Researched and collected data for a 1-week study on the Santa Cruz Island.
- Investigated existence and population of invertebrae in the Caprillidae family in Morro Bay.
- Gained thorough knowledge of identification of marine species while studying at the Washington Institute of Marine Biology. Projects included:
  - Preparing study skins of marine birds.
  - Reconstructing bone skeletons of marine fish and mammals.

EMPLOYMENT HISTORY

Cashier, Von's Grocery Store, Los Angeles, CA	1988-present
Documentation Clerk, Hughes Aircraft, El Segundo, CA	Summer 1987
Assistant Manager, Hi-Valley Development Inc, Seattle, WA	Summers 1985-86

PHILLIP T. ALEXIS

<u>Current Address</u>
666 College Place
Westwood Village, CA 90024
(213) 968-1538

<u>Permanent Address</u>
888 Circle Drive
Costa Mesa, CA 92626
(714) 555-1111

Objective: A summer Internship in the Finance Industry.

PROFESSIONAL PROFILE

- Gained valuable experience in financial analysis, sales and management while attending college to earn degree.
- Developed strong computerized research & problem solving skills.
- Dependable, conscientious and detail oriented.
- Member of the Investment Club at UCLA.

EDUCATION

BA Degree, Economics, Emphasis: Finance
<u>University of California</u>, Los Angeles, CA
Graduation: Spring 1989

RELATED EXPERIENCE

<u>Related Courses</u>
Gained valuable knowledge in Corporate Finance, Financial Accounting, Calculus, Micro/Macro Economic Theory, statistics, and Econometrics.

<u>Research & Analysis Projects</u>
- Assist professor/investment advisor with college projects.
  - Conduct in-depth computerized research to evaluate investment portfolios.
  - Research market conditions affecting current & future financial strategies.
- Learned to build financial model development and to follow the market closely using financial publications.
- Gained vital computer skills using the IBM PC with Lotus 1-2-3 software.

<u>Management & Administration</u>
- Developed marketing strategies for effective newspaper & media advertising.
- Train and supervise a staff of 20 employees, displaying strong leadership skills while maintaining a highly professional attitude.
- Successfully maintained inventory control, shipping and receiving demonstrated the ability to work well under pressure with attention to detail.

EMPLOYMENT HISTORY

Waiter, <u>The Harbor Yacht Club</u>, Seattle, WA — Summer 1987
Manager, <u>Big Sam's Restaurant</u>, Los Angeles, CA — Summer 1986

KATHRYN T. GREEN
264 D Laurel Walk
Boise, ID 98750
(208) 999-2345

Objective: Chemical Dependency and Marriage, Family & Child Counselor

PROFESSIONAL EXPERIENCE

Marriage, Family & Child Counseling
- Provided crisis intervention, brief and long term counseling to:
   -individual adults -adolescents -couples -families -groups
- Dealt with clients of diverse backgrounds in life transitions, suicide and eating disorders.
- Conducted group therapy series focused on maturation stages for early teens. Coordinated parent participation, guest speakers, field trips & written exercises.
- Served as primary crisis, individual and group counselor to emotionally disturbed teens living in a licensed group home.

Chemical Dependency Counseling & Assessment
- Counseled couples, individuals, families and adult children of alcoholics during their participation in a 12-step program.
- Primary educator on predictable course of early recovery for clients and student population.
- Instructed on indicators of potential relapse. Designed and implemented more effective treatment program, focusing on coping styles pertinent to the individual's social support system, workplace and family.

Student Personnel Services in Higher Education
- Provided individual career and developmental counseling to college students.
- Conducted eating disorder groups for the college level population.
- Multimodal case management, including video taping and presentation.
- Eating Disorders Task Force--case staffing for team of university and community professionals including psychiatrists, dietitian, individual & group therapist and eating disorder assessment & referral specialists.

SPECIAL TRAINING
- California MFCC intern license #IMF14356.
- 1-year certification program in **Alcohol & Drug** Counseling Skills - UC Santa Barbara.
- 1-year extensive **Family Therapy** training with California Center for Clinical Training and Open Systems Unlimited.
- Currently participating in 3-year **Gestalt** training program; Isabel Fredericson of the Cleveland Gestalt Institute.
- 6-month extensive training on Mental Research Institute's Model of **Brief Therapy**.
- Attended 5-day/weekend workshops - Carl Whitaker, Jay Haley and Ivan Boszormenyi-Nagy and Salvador Minuchin.
- Full caseload; 2-years, non-profit internship at Santa Barbara Night Counseling Center with weekly supervision group.

SPECIAL TRAINING (Continued)

- Full caseload at second non-profit internship <u>UC Santa Barbara</u> with weekly individual and group supervision.
- Intensive training workshop in **Focusing Technique**.
- 4-month program; interpersonal communication skills and **Transactional Analysis** therapy model-<u>Support Group Network</u>.

EMPLOYMENT HISTORY

Counselor, <u>UC Santa Barbara Counseling & Careers Center</u>	1988-present
Counselor, <u>Santa Barbara Night Counseling Center</u>	1987-present
Counselor, <u>Rivendell Group Home</u>, Santa Barbara, CA	Fall-Winter 1988
Group Counselor, <u>Santa Barbara Girl's Club</u>	Winter 1987
Counselor, <u>Ray E. Hosford Training Clinic</u>, UCSB	1986-87

PROFESSIONAL PROFILE

- Active member of Overeaters Anonymous.
- Active member of 12-Step Programs dealing with codependent relationships.
- Facilitator and member of Support Group Network.
- 3-year member in good standing; American Psychological Association.
- Member in good standing; California Association of Marriage and Family Therapists.
- Personal Psychotherapy for six years, including Family Therapy Gestalt Group Therapy, Cognitive/Behavioral, Strategic, Rogerian.

EDUCATION

- <u>MA Degree - Counseling Psychology</u>, UC Santa Barbara, June 1989 Student Personnel Services in Higher Education
- <u>Alcohol & Drug Counseling, Certificate</u>, UC Santa Barbara, June 1989
- <u>MA Degree - Counseling Psychology</u>, UC Santa Barbara, June 1988 Marriage, Family and Child Counseling
- <u>BS Degree - Psychology</u>, Cum Laude, University of Idaho, ID, 1986

SANDI R. ORION
PO Box 2345
Santa Barbara, CA 93100
(805) 888-6789

OBJECTIVE
A <u>Post-Production</u> position in the <u>Television/Film Industry</u>.

PROFESSIONAL PROFILE
- Experienced in film production/post-production management.
- Highly organized, dedicated with a positive attitude.
- Strength in assessing people's needs and priorities.
- Outstanding ability to communicate with all types of people.
- Team player with proven leadership qualities.
- Ability to handle multiple assignments in highly pressured situations and consistently meet tight deadline schedules.
- Traveled extensively throughout Japan, China, Europe, Canada, Mexico and the USA.

EDUCATION
BA Degree, Motion Picture - Spring 1990
<u>Brooks Institute of Photography</u>, Santa Barbara, CA

PRODUCTION EXPERIENCE
- Gained valuable knowledge and skills working closely with director and producer in all phases of film production.
  - Produced, directed, wrote and edited films; mixed sound tracks for several small narrative and documentary film productions.
- In charge of post-production; completed projects while consistently maintaining tight deadline schedules and strict budget requirements.

FILM & VIDEO PROJECTS
- <u>Producer</u> - "Freedom", a 15-minute documentary on the Homeless.
- <u>1st Assistant Camera</u> - "Circles", a rock style music video.
- <u>Head Editor</u> - "The Third World", a 15-minute documentary on Indonesia.
- <u>Script & Post-Production Supervisor</u>, "Non Compos Mentis", a 15-minute dramatic short. Psychological heart-beating thriller.
- <u>Assistant Camera/Editor</u> - "The Long Summer", aired on NBC Summer 1989; a documentary about a sporty homebuilt airplane.
- <u>Producer</u> - "Rhythms", an animated 3-minute music video.

References & Portfolio
Available upon request

DENISE L. LANDON
333 Austin Street
Santa Barbara, CA 93043
(805) 222-5678

OBJECTIVE
Research Assistant, Clerk or Writer/Editor for a Law Firm.

PROFESSIONAL PROFILE
- Developed excellent skills in legal writing and research.
- Outstanding ability to communicate with all types of people.
- Work well under pressure; thrive on challenging projects.
- Ranked in the Top 10 of first year students in law school.

EDUCATION
JD, <u>Los Angeles College of Law</u>
Graduation: December 1991

Law-Related Courses

Legal Writing & Research...Criminal Law...Criminal Procedure ...Contracts...Torts...Juvenile Law...Family Law...Wills & Trusts...Personal Property...Real Property...Civil Procedures ...Dispute Resolution...Bioethics

RELATED EXPERIENCE

Research Writing & Communication Skills
- Wrote/submitted a client history on behalf of a Cuban detainee at LA Federal Prison.
  - Contacted client's family to verify USA sponsorship.
  - Researched extensive criminal record.
  - Represented and counseled client at an INS deportation hearing.
- Researched and wrote a summary on the origins of Canons of Legal Ethics.
- Participant in a thorough research project to establish a curriculum for the Los Angeles College of Law Writing and Research class.

Project Coordination/Management
- Prepared income tax returns in conjunction with the IRS and the Volunteer Income Tax Assistance Program.
- Managed a major grocery store; hired, trained and supervised 2-120 employees.
- Oversaw the entire budget; Increased annual profits by 98 percent within the first year.
- Developed and coordinated an effective employee training manual and video.
  - Wrote, directed, casted and introduced the scanner system to 25,000 employees.

EMPLOYMENT HISTORY

Manager/Bookkeeper, <u>Albertson's Market</u>, Long Beach   1978-present

SUSAN E. PERLMAN
39 Wilcox Lane
Ft Collins, CO 80521
(303) 671-4798

Objective: Research Historian

EDUCATION

MA Degree, History, 1990
New Mexico State University, Las Cruces, NM
Master's Thesis: "Livestock Policy of the Zuni
Indian Tribe: 1900-1942

Paralegal Certificate, 1983
Denver Paralegal Institute, Denver, CO

BS Degree, Environmental Interpretation, 1979
Colorado State University, Fort Collins, CO

PAPERS PRESENTED

"New Deal at Zuni: The Range Management Program,"
Historical Society of New Mexico, Annual Conference, April, 1990

"Zuni Indian Livestock Policy During the Early Twentieth Century,"
Historical Society of New Mexico, Annual Conference, 1989.

"Apache Scouts and the United States Army,"
Phi Alpha Theta Regional Conference, 1988.

PROFESSIONAL EXPERIENCE

Research: Historical & Technical
- Prepared reports on natural resource utilization on Indian lands in New Mexico and Arizona.
  - Researched government documents, regulations, serials, archives, secondary sources.
  - Compiled, abstracted, and analyzed raw data.
  - Performed title searches in county and federal records.
- Coordinated court exhibits and data tables prepare for submission of land claims report.
- Conducted historical research projects as a graduate research assistant.
- Performed legal research and administration of law library.
- Conducted technical research in the following fields:
  forestry...agriculture...animal husbandry...and hydrology.

- More -

PROFESSIONAL EXPERIENCE (Continued)

Writing: Historical & Technical

- Wrote reports on Native American land and water utilization and rights for litigation use.
- Assembled annotated bibliographies for economic and resource study.
- Drafted pleadings for real estate, litigation, and estate administration.
- Composed and maintained correspondence with clients.Communication Experience
- Conducted extensive oral interviews; interviewees included Native American prison inmates, Native American livestock producers, alumnae for university centennial, legal and social services clients.
- Served as liaison between Native American self-help group and prison administration.
- Initiated development of cooperative programs with government agencies and community organizations.
- Worked closely with local, state, federal agencies and community groups.
- Established US Forest Service Visitor Center; responsible for development of exhibits.

Technical Experience

- Operate computers for database, writing, research, file management, and abstracting.
- Skilled interpreter of photographs and topographic maps.
- Maintained timber inventory and timber sale layout.
- Supervised timber field crews.

EMPLOYMENT HISTORY

Historian, <u>Historical Research Associates</u>, Missoula, Montana	1989-present
Sponsor, <u>Native American Council</u>, Southern New Mexico Correctional Facility, Las Cruces, NM	1988-89
Research Assist, <u>Institute of North American West</u>, Albuquerque, NM	1988
History Research/Teaching Assistant, <u>New Mexico State University</u>	1987-89
Medicaid Elig Tech, <u>Larimer Cty-Social Serv</u>, Ft Collins, CO	1984-86
Legal Sec/Paralegal, <u>Remington Plaza Law Offices</u>, Ft Collins, CO	1984
Paralegal Intern, <u>Environmental Defense fund</u>, Boulder, CO	1983
Forestry Tech, <u>US Forest Service</u>, Ft Collins, CO	1979-81

MAX RYAN MICHAELSON

Current Address
6222 Riverview Road, Apt E
Boulder, CO 80524
(303) 251-1278

Permanent Address
20341 Raymond Street
Portland, OR 97039
(202) 315-9346

Objective: A Mechanical Engineering Internship

EDUCATION

BS Degree, Mechanical Engineering, June 1991
University of Colorado, Boulder, CO

RELATED EXPERIENCE

Printer Operator Technician
- Operated Xerox 9700 Laser printers for a computer company.
  - Repaired complex mechanical computer systems and printers, meeting strict deadline schedules on a daily basis; performed data entry on the IBM PC computer.
- Learned to work on multiple assignments under pressured situations while maintaining a positive attitude.

Communication & Organization Skills
- Picked up tapes, printed information/delivered tapes from Denver to Boulder, CO.
  - Liaison and main source of information between clients and management staff at two locations for a very service-oriented company.
  - Maintained excellent communications with managers of major corporations to meet tight deadline requirements.
- Prepared displays & software packages for national trade show exhibitions.
- Gained vital organizational and communication skills.

Public Speaking & Promotions
- Led tours throughout the UC Boulder campus to high school students and parents.
- Successfully promoted dorm attendance & activities for 1000 dorm students.
  - Interviewed students and reviewed personal information forms to evaluate and determine living situations.
  - Guided tours and provided assistance to students for the facility.
- Learned to speak in front of large and small groups of people in a highly professional manner with poise and dignity.

EMPLOYMENT HISTORY

Office Assistant, Tropicana Gardens, Boulder, CO	1989-present
Tour Guide, UC Boulder, (Relations with Schools Dept)	Spring 1988
Printer Operator/Technician, X-Tec Systems, Boulder, CO	1984-87

MANDY LISA LENNON

Current Address	**Permanent Address**
6661 Shannon Place	11th Avenue
Santa Barbara, CA 93103	Bellingham, WA 99353
(805) 967-0869	(202) 382-4587

OBJECTIVE
A growth-oriented Urban Development position

EDUCATION
BA Degree, Sociology, December 1989
University of California, Santa Barbara

RELATED EXPERIENCE

Communication Skills
- Educate the Greek community and the entire UCSB campus to promote racial awareness and cultural sensitivity.
  - Received intensive professional training to facilitate programs.
- Speak with poise and confidence in front of large/small groups of people.
- Interfaced via phone with clients worldwide for a large financial institution.
- Learned to maintain a highly professional and concerned manner under sensitive situations.

Organization & Administrative Skills
- Established procedures for GRACE as part of a 20-member team.
- Planned and supervised daily activities for 20 children ages 6-7 at a cultural day camp in Seattle, WA. Oversaw associate counselors.
  - Created programs focusing on a wide range of cultures each week.
- Coordinated a large Philanthropy event for the American Cancer Society and Diabetes Foundation. In charge of ticket distribution and sales.
  - Successfully promoted fundraiser through local business sponsorship.
- Prepared daily bookkeeping procedures for a large international bank.
- Learned to work on multiple projects under pressured situations and consistently meet strict deadline schedules.

HONORS/ACTIVITIES
Excellence in Public Relations Award
Executive Planning Committee, Philanthropy
GRACE Rep., Cultural Awareness Program
Social Chair, Chi Omega Pledge Class
Spirit Chair, Chi Omega Sorority

EMPLOYMENT HISTORY
Assistant Bookkeeper, Wells Fargo Asian Bank, Seattle, WA	Summer 1988
Head Counselor, Friendship Day Camp, Seattle, WA	Summer 1987

MOLLY RACHEL KANTRELL
567 Gold Hill Road
Boulder, CO 80309
(303) 492-0736

OBJECTIVE
A growth-oriented Executive Sales/Marketing position

SKILLS

ORGANIZATION

- Delegated jobs to work committees, planned and managed all activities, and set standards for the smooth running of a sorority as the president.
- Composed press releases, assembled press kits and collected data for an advertising campaign for the Boulder Museum of Art.
- Implemented programs designed to promote scholastic achievement within college sorority, resulted in presentation of Scholastic Excellence Award by the Panhellenic Council.
- Scheduled and assisted in fundraising events, assembled press clippings and wrote press releases for the Heart Association as an intern.

COMMUNICATION

- Acted as a liaison between active and alumni members and promoted sorority activities both within the chapter and in various other settings through public speaking events as an executive sorority officer.
- Worked with customers assisting them with their cameras and photographs, and informed the public about upcoming sales and new merchandise as a camera shop sales associate.
- Implemented new Public Relations programs, working closely with the Boulder Museum of Art Public Relations/Development Dept.
- Operated communication systems between office volunteers and staff of the Heart Association as an intern.

EDUCATION
BA Degree, Communication Studies, 12-89
University of Colorado, Boulder, CO

HONORS AND EXPERIENCE
- **President/Vice-president**, Chi Omega Sorority, 1987-89
- **Outstanding Senior Award**, Chi Omega Sorority, June 1989
- **Sales Associate**, Cañada Camera Shop, Boulder, CO, 1983-87
- **Grants & Public Relations Intern**, Boulder Museum of Art, 1989
- **Public Relations Intern**, Boulder County Chapter, American Heart Association, 1988

KATY AMANDA CARTER
Peachtree Lane
Atlanta, GA 30179
(312) 459-2301

Objective: A Research Assistant for a Biotech firm

EDUCATION

BS Degree, Bio-Psychology, Summer 1990
University of Georgia, Athens, GA

RELATED EXPERIENCE

Related Courses
Physiological Psychology...Psychopharmacology...Hormones & Behavior..Sensory Processes...Pharmacology...Pharmacology Lab...Experimental Psychology Lab...Physics...Biology...Chemistry...Organic Chemistry...Statistics.

Bio-Psychology Research Lab
- Researched and collected data for a Ph.D. graduate student's Master Thesis.
  - Set up and performed laboratory experiments on a daily basis for a year.
  - Injected laboratory animals, measured oxygen consumption and body temperature change to investigate the effects of drugs on thermogenesis.
- Gained valuable knowledge of research and surgery techniques in a bio-psychology lab setting including...
  - stereotaxic surgery, cannula implants, electrolytic lesions, adrenalectomy.
- Trained and supervised other volunteer research assistants with the entire lab set up and proper experimental procedures.

HONORS/ACTIVITIES

Member, Psi-Chi, National Psychology Honor Society
Member, Alpha Lambda Delta, Freshman Honor Society
Personnel Officer, Chi Omega Sorority UG
Alumni/Out-of-House Relations, Chi Omega Sorority, UG

WORK HISTORY

Research Volunteer, University of Georgia, Athens, GA	1988-present
Waitress/Shift Leader, Cajon Station, Atlanta, GA	1987-88
Library Assistant, University of Georgia Library, Athens, GA	1986-87

NICOLE E. DANSEN

Campus Address
25689 Rhino Street
Goleta, CA 93117
(805) 966-3049

Permanent Address
207 Oceanside Road
Corona Del Mar, CA 92625
(714) 644-5091

Objective: Law Clerk

EDUCATION

BA Degree, Law and Society, June 1991
University of California, Santa Barbara

EXPERIENCE

Related Courses
Law in Modern State...American Government and Politics...Law and Society... Critical Thinking...Sociology of Law...Criminal Justice... Constitutional Law.

Public Relations/Communications
- Greeted clientele and answered busy phones for a 10-attorney law firm expediting challenges customers presented in a highly professional manner.
  - Assisted attorneys quickly and efficiently maintaining tact and diplomacy.
- Demonstrated strong public relation skills while waitressing for two service-oriented sandwich shops.
  - Developed a personal customer base through excellent customer service, and thorough product knowledge.
  - Trained and supervised waitress personnel.
- Learned to work well with employees, clients and all levels of management.

Administrative Skills
- Operated computer for a law firm to convert manual procedures to computerized office system. Filed and sorted documents with accuracy and speed.
- Maintained opening/closing procedures as well as cash management at two restaurants.
- Learned to work on multiple projects under highly pressured situations and consistently meet strict deadline schedules.

EMPLOYMENT HISTORY

Waitress/Hostess, Cafe Del Mar, San Diego, CA	Summer/Winter 1988-90
Waitress, Matinee Bar and Grill, Irvine, CA	1986-88
Office Assistant, Law Offices of Dansen & Pram, Irvine, CA	1985-86

LAURA K. ALEXANDRIA

Current Address	**Permanent Address**
45 Triego Avenue	222 Circle Lane
Goleta, CA 93117	Oceanside, CA 92667
(805) 555-1111	(619) 222-1111

OBJECTIVE: **A Public Relations position in the Broadcast Industry.**

PROFILE:
- Financed education with experience in sales and management.
- Highly organized, dedicated with a positive attitude.
- Excellent written, oral and interpersonal communication skills.
- Problem solver/team player with proven leadership qualities.
- Traveled throughout Europe, Asia, India, Japan, Russia, USA.

EDUCATION: **BA Degree, Communications**
University of California, Los Angeles
Graduation: June 1989   GPA: 3.5

EXPERIENCE:

1988-89   **News Assistant Intern**, ABC Television, Los Angeles, CA
- Assisted the entire news broadcast management and staff.
- Wrote documentaries and news coverage.
- Teleprompt for the news staff during broadcasting.
- Coordinated advertising and processed extensive mass mailings on a weekly basis; consistently met demanding deadlines.
- Contacted public service throughout the Santa Barbara Tri-County area to provide information for news staff.
- Position requires the ability to handle multiple assignments under pressured situations quickly and efficiently.

Fall 1987   **Rush Counselor**, UC Los Angeles, CA
- Counseled 20 girls in the UCLA Sorority Rush Program.
- Set up/conducted stress management and problem solving meetings.
- Demonstrated strong leadership skills with the ability to maintain a positive attitude in highly pressured situations.

ACTIVITIES:
- Alumni Relations Committee member
- Rush Counselor
- Alumni Representative
- Philanthropy Volunteer

HAYLEY LENNON

2345 College Drive, Washington, DC 90210   (212) 222-9090

OBJECTIVE: Desire further education and training in <u>Child Development</u>.

EDUCATION: **Bachelor of Arts - Psychology with Honors**
<u>Georgetown University</u>, Washington, DC
Graduation: June 1990   GPA: 3.9

**ACADEMIC
HONORS:**   Dean's List of Scholastic Excellence
1987 to 1989 (7 times)

EXPERIENCE:

1988-89   **GROUP HOME RESIDENTIAL INTERN**
<u>The Home Group</u>, Fairfax, VA
- Provide counseling and support for emotionally disturbed and/or juvenile delinquent female residents of a teenage group home.
- Assist staff in program planning and implementation.
- Attend weekly supervision meetings conducted by a licensed Marriage, Family & Child Counselor.

1987-89   **RESIDENTIAL AID**
<u>The Child's Foundation</u>, Fairfax, VA
- Assisted with behavior modification and independent living programs.
- Implement programs for developmentally disabled males ages 15-23.
- Increased effective counseling and conflict intervention skills.

1986-87   **RESEARCH ASSISTANT**
<u>Goergetown University</u>, Washington, DC
Department of Psychology, Dr. H.P. Samuels
- Prepared subjects for participation in research projects.
- Assisted in data collection that examined interpersonal processes and social interactions.

1985-86   **PRE-SCHOOL TEACHER**
<u>The Children's Center</u>, Fairfax, VA
- Prepared children with necessary developmental skills.
- Acquired planning and scheduling techniques.
- Increased communication skills through the use of conflict negotiation with children ages 2-1/2 to 6 years old.

KATHRYN A. JULIANA
444 College Avenue
Goleta, CA 93117
(805) 555-1234

Objective: A position leading to Public Relations career

PROFESSIONAL PROFILE: Success oriented with high energy and a positive attitude... strong sense of responsibility and self motivation...good written and oral communication skills...great problem solver and team player with the ability to work independently...creative, flexible and efficient.

EDUCATION: **BA Degree - Public Relations - 1991**
University of California, Los Angeles, CA

Study of the Arts, Paris, France - 1987
American Institute for Foreign Studies

PROFESSIONAL EXPERIENCE:

Summer 1989 **PUBLIC AFFAIRS INTERN**, General Hospital, Los Angeles, CA
- Wrote and edited press releases for local media and articles for in-house weekly newsletters and quarterly magazines.
- Developed successful advertising campaigns to promote major fund raising events; worked closely with TV, newspaper and radio news media.
- Created and designed effective brochures and flyers utilizing the desktop publishing system.

Fall 1988 **PUBLIC RELATIONS INTERN**, CBS Television, Los Angeles, CA
- Wrote and published effective newspaper advertising copy, press releases and letters to the business community.
- Developed marketing strategies to promote television services and sponsor community events throughout Santa Barbara.
- Learned research skills, writing techniques and the ability to communicate effectively with professionals of all levels.

Winter 1987 **SALES ASSISTANT**, Bullock's Department Store, Los Angeles, CA
- Persuasion and promotional skills used in product sales.
- Innovation to create new displays.
- Disciplined time management in a 50 hour work week.
- Active listening and professionalism employed in customer service and employee relations.

SCOTT RAYMOND JOHNSON

9912 Media Road, Los Angeles, California 93111   (213) 964-3599

OBJECTIVE: **An entry level Biologist position.**

EDUCATION: **Biological Sciences/Biochemistry, 1987-88**
University of California at Los Angeles

Marine Science Program, Certified 1985-87
Los Angeles City College, Los Angeles

PADI Certification - Rescue Diver, 1986
CPR/AR Red Cross Certification, 1986

SUMMARY OF EXPERIENCE:
UNIVERSITY OF CALIFORNIA, Los Angeles, CA   Winter 1988
Chemistry Storeroom Assistant
• Maintained supply of chemicals for graduate research.
• Assisted graduate students for the set-up of chemical apparatus.
• Responsible for liquid Nitrogen/Acetone accessibility and tank operation.
• Validated cost center codes for input into computer.

LOS ANGELES CITY COLLEGE, Los Angeles, CA   1986-87
Mathematics Tutor
• Evaluated material for classroom of 20 students.
• Counseled students on an individual basis to promote effective learning skills.
• Graded exams and homework material to evaluate student progress.
• Available for tutoring on a one-on-one basis outside of classroom instruction.

SEA WORLD, San Diego, CA
Safety & Maintenance Technician/Tour Guide   Summers 1984-85
• Prepared Hydrofoils for daily readiness.
• Performed hydraulic, oil, fuel, coolant system and transmission testing to assure proper functioning of engine and boat.
• Evaluated systems check and passenger safety via log entries for each trip.
• Answered questions pertaining to sea life and boat operation.
• Guided visitors to park exhibits.

HONORS
• Won Chamber of Commerce Sports and Attractions Committee Award.

JIM ANTONIO
7770 Landre Lane
Santa Barbara, CA 93101
(805) 555-1123

EDITORIAL PHOTOGRAPHER

EDUCATION: **BA Degree, Illustration Photography, 1988**
Brooks Institute of Photography, Santa Barbara

PHOTOGRAPHY SKILLS: Gained a broad range of knowledge and skills in special techniques and still life, concept development, location/studio and set building. Strongly emphasize editorial and fashion photography.

- Experience with 35mm, 2-1/4, 4x5 and 8/10 cameras.
- Professionally capable of lighting with Balcar, Tungsten, Norman, Speedatron strobes and audio visual equipment to produce slide shows.
- Extensive knowledge of printing, black & white, kodalith, duping, and flat art copy films.

CLIENTS/ PROJECTS: **Alexis Productions** - Selected to photograph "Fall Vision", the annual fashion show for merchants in the Montecito and Santa Barbara area. 1986-87.

Santa Barbara Independent - Photographed a variety of editorial work for the style section of this popular weekly news and entertainment newspaper. Summer 1988

DeMarcos Modeling Agency - Photographed fashion models for test shooting. Selected models, choose clothing, accessories and set scenes for a theme or to create the environment. 1986-88

EMPLOYMENT:

Spring 1988 HENDRY'S STUDIOS, Santa Barbara, CA
Internship
- Assisted the illustration photographer in all phases of commercial photography for this busy studio.
- Sharpened my technical skills and creative ability while working well under tight deadline schedules.

1986-88 BROOKS INSTITUTE OF PHOTOGRAPHY, Santa Barbara, CA
Technical Assistant
- Assisted students in the producing slide shows in the Audio Visual Dept.

THOMAS W. CHESCA

Current Address:
100 Freedom Court
Santa Barbara, CA 93101
(805) 666-2345

Permanent Address:
123 Los Sierra Drive
San Diego, CA 94444
(619) 222-7999

Objective: A <u>Paralegal</u> position with a law firm.

EDUCATION
BA Degree, Law and Society
<u>University of California</u>, Los Angeles
Graduation: December 1987

LEGAL EXPERIENCE
LA COUNTY MUNICIPAL COURT, Los Angeles, CA   1985-present
Legal Research Assistant
- Conduct research and prepare notes for small claims court.
- Gather information for cases under submission.
- Survey and study areas under dispute.
- Contact various individuals on behalf of court to gather additional information for proper court ruling.
- Diagram areas under question.
- Type final reports and present them to the commissioner.

LA COUNTY, OWN RECOGNIZANCE UNIT, Los Angeles, CA   1983-84
Court Services Investigator
- Interviewed pre-trial felony detainees and conducted background investigations to determine eligibility for release, bail reduction or elevation.
- Wrote reports to explain why the alleged felon was granted or denied an OR release, which becomes a legal document.
- Grant conditional releases with recommendation for alcohol and/or drug abuse treatment and family violence counseling.
- Contact and acquire input from prosecuting/defense attorney's, law enforcement agencies (Police, FBI, Probation Departments), judges and victims.
- Recruited and trained student interns.
- Required objectivity and responsibility under restriction of confidentiality.

EMPLOYMENT HISTORY
Waiter, <u>The Whales Tail Restaurant</u>, Newport Beach, CA   Summer 1986
Swim Instructor, <u>LA Swim Club</u>, Los Angeles, CA   Summers 1981-82
Windsurfing Instructor, <u>The Sport Club</u>, Los Angeles, CA   Summer 1980

SUSAN M. ALLEN
1251 26th Avenue
Bellingham, WA 22220
(202) 777-1234

SALES MANAGER/REPRESENTATIVE

PROFESSIONAL OBJECTIVE:

Seeking a reputable company offering salary based on individual contributions to goals.

PROFESSIONAL PROFILE:

Success oriented and competitive with high energy and a positive mental attitude...strong sense of responsibility and self motivation...good written and oral communication skills...great problem solver and team player with proven leadership qualities... enthusiastic...creative...flexible and efficient work habits.

SALES EXPERIENCE:

1982-present **SALES ASSOCIATE**, Sears Department Store, Santa Barbara, CA.
- Consistent award winner and top percent over goal of maintenance agreements for the entire store.
- Successfully generate and maintain new business with thorough product knowledge in the Appliance, Men's Clothing and Shoe departments meeting deadlines on a daily basis.
- Help customers make satisfactory buying decisions while developing a large personal customer base, involving maintenance agreement sales and customer follow up.
- Demonstrated effective problem solving skills, expediting challenges customers present in a quick and creative manner.

1988-present **MARKETING REPRESENTATIVE**
Market Source Corporation, Cranbury, NJ.
- Set up booths to promote products of major charge card, food, corporations nationwide.
- Work closely with the University of California and real estate agencies throughout the Tri-County.
- Consistently meet company quota of promotions and sales.

EDUCATION: **BA Degree - Physical Education/Health, 1988**
Westmont College, Santa Barbara, CA

HANNAH SPIELBERG
234 Gayley Avenue
Westwood, CA 90024
(213) 360-1234

OBJECTIVE
An Art Historian/Research position for a museum

EDUCATION
BA Degree - Art History, 1991
University of California, Los Angeles

WORK EXPERIENCE

UCLA Daily Bruin, 1989-present
Staff writer. Review local art exhibitions and conduct personal interviews with artists for the Arts and Entertainment Section.

UCLA Art Museum Docent and Educator, 1988-89
Tour Guide. Guided tours of exhibitions at the museum to students and adults. Involved in the art education/outreach programs entailing instructing children from kindergarten through third grade in painting and sculpture.

Contemporary Arts Forum Home Shop, Fall 1988
Lecturer. Volunteered every Sunday for one-month at the installation by Joseph Kosuth. Developed an understanding of Kosuth's work and provided such information to viewers.

Earthwatch Expedition, August 1987
Archeologist. Selected to participate in a one-month expedition conducted by the University of Arizona in Winslow, AZ. The expedition involved excavating a native American Indian site. Learned valuable skills archeological techniques and knowledge in native Indian arts with emphasis in pottery.

AWARDS/MEMBERSHIPS
- UCLA Art History Affiliate Award 1989
- Dean's Honor List 1987-89 (3-times)
- UCLA Art History Honor's Program
- Outstanding College Students of America
- Golden Key National Honors Society
- Contemporary Arts Forum, Los Angeles
- Museum of Contemporary Art, Los Angeles

EMPLOYMENT HISTORY
Waitress, Hamburger Hamlet, Westwood, CA   1987-90
Waitress, Yesterday's Bar & Grill, Westwood, CA   1983-1986

ANNIE LINDSEY
34518 Beverly Glen
Los Angeles, CA 90024
(213) 567-1238

Objective: A Systems Programmer position

COMPUTER SKILLS
<u>Languages</u>: "C" Pascal, Fortran, Prolog, 8088 Assembly
<u>Software/Hardware</u>: UNIX, MS-DOS, IBM, Macintosh, VAX

EDUCATION
BS Degree, Mathematical Science, 1990
<u>University of California</u>, Los Angeles

CURRENT PROFESSIONAL EXPERIENCE
DARCY CORPORATION, Los Angeles, CA   1989-present
(A pension software development manufacturer)
Software Support Specialist
- Liaison between 400 customers and seven computer programmers.
  - Consult customers and troubleshoot data management and pension software systems.
  - Certify and test new software packages.
- Required strong analytical and written skills with ability to communicate well with clients, fellow employees and all levels of management.

Software Development Certification
- Developed several effective testing procedures on the IBM computer for three pension plans in Expert systems.
- Wrote extensive testing reports; reported directly to the Vice President.
- Received thorough training in pensions participant eligibility.
- After 3-month internship progressed to full-time Software Certification.

ACTIVITIES
Member, <u>Society of Women Engineers</u>

PREVIOUS EMPLOYMENT HISTORY
Mathematics Lab Assistant, <u>UC Los Angeles</u>, (Math Dept)   1987-88
Billing Assistant, <u>UC Los Angeles</u>, (Billing Office)   1986-87

NICOLAS ANTHONY
2367 Gold Hill
Nederlands, CO 80534
(303) 345-6789

Objective: A Design Engineer position.

EDUCATION:

BS Degree, Physics, March 1991
University of Colorado, Boulder, CO

AA Degree, Engineering, 1985
Santa Barbara City College, Santa Barbara, CA

AS Degree, Aviation Maintenance, 1984
Santa Barbara City College, Santa Barbara, CA

JOB EXPERIENCE:

1989-present RESEARCH WEST CORPORATION, Boulder, CO
Engineering Aid I
- Assist engineers in design, testing, and implementation of instrumentation for various energy measurement experiments.
- Design and fabricate apparatus for materials testing on vacuum.
- Start up and maintenance of class 100 clean room.
- Perform mechanical design using computer aided drafting (CAD).
- Programmed computer using FORTRAN and BASIC languages.
- Setup electrical tests i.e., oscilloscopes, meters, power supplies.

1986-89 AVIATION CORPORATION, Carpinteria, CA
Aircraft Inspector
- Performed heavy inspections (C and D checks) on the following aircraft: DC-10 (-30, -40) 727 -200, DC-9 (-10, -30, -40, -50).
- Inspect installations and modifications of structural, electrical, and hydraulic systems on DC-10 (-30, -40), 747-SP, MD-80.
- Performed heavy maintenance on McDonnell Douglas DC-10 aircraft, including engine and flight control replacements.
- Repaired and modified aircraft systems and components.
- Trained and supervised apprentice mechanics.

1980-86 WEST COAST AIRLINES, Santa Maria, CA, CA
Quality Control Inspector
- Inspected aircraft repairs and required inspection items (RII).
- Accomplished checks on aircraft and engines.
- Designed tooling for maintenance applications.
- Performed nondestructive testing methods including magnaflux, eddy current and dye penetrant; trained new inspectors.

NATASHA LAKINSKI

Present Address
1345 Wisconsin Avenue
Washington DC 01003
(202) 470-0021

Permanent Address
Springfield Drive
Berkeley, CA 93902
(415) 234-9876

Objective: A position leading to a career in Broadcasting

EDUCATION: **BA Degree, Communication Studies**, June 1989
George Washington University, Washington, DC

Related Coursework
Interpersonal/Small Group Communication   Rhetoric & Phonetics
Public Communication   Mass Communication
Communication and Conflict   Persuasion

**BROADCASTING
EXPERIENCE:** **PRODUCTION/REPORTER INTERN,**
Channel 22, Government Access, Fairfax, VA

1988-90 Studio Production
• Assisted production staff for a weekly talk show.
   - Operated cameras...floor directed...set-up lighting equipment.
   - Prepared sets before and in-between tapings.
   - Supervised camera operators during talk shows.

Field Production
• Researched/reported three 180 second news packages aired on public television.
   - Wrote and edited scripts; operated video cameras.
• Learned how to handle multiple assignments under highly pressured situations quickly and efficiently.

Talk Show Host
• Hosted weekly talk shows concerning the local community.
   - family issues...safety programs...recreational activities.
• Learned to speak with poise and confidence in front of camera.
• Gained valuable research skills, writing techniques and the ability to communicate effectively with professionals at all levels.

ACTIVITIES: **PRESIDENT**, University Advertising Club, 1987-88
In charge of coordinating and conducting weekly meetings. Organized guest speakers. Created a learning environment for students eager to learn about the advertising industry.

NADIA NATALIA GAVIN
126 Anapamu Street
Santa Barbara, CA 93101
(805) 985-8765

OBJECTIVE: A <u>Sales Management Trainee</u> position.

**PROFESSIONAL
PROFILE:**

- Experienced in customer relations, promotions & management.
- Highly organized, dedicated with a positive attitude.
- Proven ability to run a smooth efficient operation.
- Special talent for assessing clients needs and gaining trust.
- Thrive in a competitive and challenging environment.
- Outstanding ability to communicate with all types of people.

EDUCATION: **BA Degree, Sociology**
<u>University of California</u>, Santa Barbara
Graduation: Summer 1991

EXPERIENCE:

1989-90   ALBERTSONS INC, Santa Barbara, CA
Checker/Cashier
- Demonstrate strong customer relation skills through daily interaction with the general public.
- Maintain and balance large volumes of cash transactions quickly and accurately on a daily basis.

1985-88   TCBY, THE COUNTRY'S BEST YOGURT, Santa Barbara, CA
Assistant Manager
In charge of entire store operations.
- Developed and implemented successful marketing strategies to promote products; design effective in-store displays.
- Conducted motivational sales meeting for all sales staff.
- Established a large customer base through excellent customer service and staff management.
- Hired, trained and supervised employees maintaining a highly professional and diplomatic manner.

Other Positions Held: retail sales in department store and courtesy clerk at a grocery store.

ACTIVITIES:
- **Jr. Executive Chairperson**, <u>Gamma Phi Beta Sorority</u>

KARLA J. KOPER
6695 Wilcox Lane
Los Angeles, CA 90024
(213) 502-3451

OBJECTIVE
An Administrative Assistant in the Medical profession

EDUCATION
BA Degree, Political Science, June 1990
University of California, Los Angeles
Dean's Honor List: Spring 1989   GPA: 3.2

Semester at Sea Program, March-June 1982
University of Pittsburgh
Around the world studies (12 countries)

CURRENT PROFESSIONAL EXPERIENCE
UCLA MEDICAL CENTER, Los Angeles, CA   1985-present
Pharmacy Technician
- In charge of work flow for 16 technicians in the pharmacy department of a busy 6-floor, 400+ bed hospital.
- Key member in converting manual procedures to a sophisticated computer system.
  - Developed effective training methods for staff members.
  - Organized/conducted training sessions for technicians and pharmacists.
- Prepared/distributed unit dose & intravenous drugs for all nursing units.
- Interpreted and clarified physicians' orders with attention to detail.
- Served as liaison between pharmacists, physicians and nurses to insure accuracy and safety of pharmaceutical procedures for patients.
- Worked on multiple projects simultaneously under highly pressured situations and consistently met strict deadline schedules.

WESTWOOD PLAZA DRUG, Westwood Village, CA   1982-85
Pharmacy Technician/Cashier/Sales
- Answered customer inquiries and developed a large personal customer base, demonstrating thorough product knowledge and excellent customer service.
- Typed prescriptions into the computer. Thoroughly familiar with medical terminology.
- Prepared claims for Medi-Cal and Health Net insurance customers.

PREVIOUS PROFESSIONAL EXPERIENCE
Administrative Assistant, UC Pittsburgh, Semister at Sea   Summer 1982
Sales Associate, Paradise Drug Store, Boulder, CO   1981-82

MEGAN RYAN ESCOBAR

Campus Address	**Permanent Address**
1704 Wilshire Blvd	201 River Ridge Springs
Los Angeles, CA 90025	Seattle, WA 10005
(213) 502-4455	(201) 525-1223

Objective: A growth-oriented position leading to a career in Law.

EDUCATION

BA Degree, Political Science, December 1990
University of California, Los Angeles

LEGAL EXPERIENCE

CAREY T. LUNDSFORD, LAW CORPORATION, Los Angeles, CA   Summer 1990
Bilingual Law Clerk
- Interviewed Spanish speaking clients and served as translator for attorney.
- Prepared extensive bankruptcy cases with efficiency.
- Filed documents with the municipal and superior courts.
- Supervised office in absence of the attorney and staff.
- Demonstrated tact and diplomacy with clients and attorney under pressured situations; consistently met strict deadline schedules.

GOVERNMENT ACCOUNTABILITY PROJECT, Washington, DC   Summer 1989
Staff Associate Intern
- Partner on 4-person team whose advocacy for whistleblowers was a leading factor in stopping USDA's proposal to restructure government's approach to food safety oversight.
- Researched/analyzed over 1800 public comments on DI, and 240 comments on the Streamlined Inspection System to deregulate slaughter inspection.
- Conducted numerous telephone inquiries and library research to identify relevant military quality control standards for contractors.
  - Information used as reference to evaluate USDA's weaker QC criteria for the food industry.
- Served as media liaison to alert and recruit reporters to attend press conferences where investigative results were disclosed.
- Conducted library research to keep abreast of how journalists were covering clients' whistleblowing disclosures in each area.
- Served as client liaison to learn if/how information could be made public.
- Conducted exhaustive advance public relations outreach for GAP-sponsored awards ceremonies honoring specific whistleblowers.

EMPLOYMENT HISTORY

Teacher's Assistant, UCLA La Escuelita Program, Westwood, CA   1988-89
Resident Assistant, UCLA Partnership Academic Institute, Westwood, CA   Summer 1988
Tutor, La Escuelita Tutoring Program, Franklin School, Los Angeles, CA   1986-88

JANICE CALDWELL

Campus Address	**Permanent Address**
6643 Sueno #A	207 Evening Canyon Road
Goleta, CA 93117	Corona Del Mar, CA 92625
(805) 562-8411	(714) 644-8018

Objective: An Internship leading to a career in Public Relations.

EDUCATION
BA Degree, Law and Society, June 1991
<u>University of California</u>, Santa Barbara

PUBLIC INTEREST EXPERIENCE

CALIFORNIA PUBLIC INTEREST RESEARCH GROUP   Santa Barbara, CA
Research Intern (Fall 1990)
- Researched and reviewed current periodicals and books pertaining to environmental energy policy and other public interest issues.
- Identified, reviewed, recommended and located new publications and articles for the resource center.
- Served as precinct leader for environmental electoral initiative campaign.
- Contacted local community through phone and door-to-door solicitation.
- Delegated, trained and supervised responsibilies to volunteer staff.
- Gained vital leadership, organization and interpersonal communication skills.

PUBLIC CITIZEN'S CRITICAL MASS ENERGY PROJECT   Washington DC
Researcher, Writer, Editor, Coordinator (Summer 1990)
- Researched/edited reports, press releases/editorials related to energy policy issues.
- Wrote a letter to Congress as part of an active lobbying campaign.
- Co-authored two published reports on pertinent energy issues.
- Worked directly with the media and national citizen groups. Learned how to communicate effectively with all levels of professionals.
- Helped organize and promote a national seminar and two press conferences.
- Consistently met demanding deadlines under highly pressured situations.

PREVIOUS EMPLOYMENT HISTORY

Wordprocessor, <u>Freelance</u>, Santa Barbara, CA	1988-present
Community Service, <u>Nat'l Charity League</u>, Newport, CA	1980-87
Office Assistant, <u>Law Offices of Kasdan</u>, Irvine, CA	1985-86

Chapter VI
COVER LETTER & THANK YOU
LETTER SAMPLES

About Cover Letters

A cover letter is simply a letter introducing you and your resume to the employer. Cover letters are needed whenever you mail your resume to an employer. They can be personalized or generalized but are written specifically to go with the individual's resume. The cover letter accompanying your resume is divided into three paragraphs.

1. The first paragraph states why you are writing, that is, what position you're applying for and whether you saw an advertisement or heard about the position or company through a referral or simply by reputation.

2. The second paragraph is a brief summary stating why you feel qualified for the position. What makes you different. If adding the Professional Profile section in a resume will make an otherwise one-page resume into two pages, I'll use it in a cover letter instead. Never use it for both or repeat exactly what is said in the resume.

3. The third paragraph is the closing statement saying where you can be reached and thanking the employer. See the following cover letter samples.

About Thank You Letters

A thank you letter is sent after you've had an interview for a position you're interested in. The thank you letter should be mailed the day of the interview; it should be brief and personalized. Follow this three-paragraph procedure:

1. In the opening paragraph simply thank the interviewer, re-emphasizing your interest in the position.

2. The second paragraph reminds the employer why you are a good candidate for the position. Try to remember something specific in the interview to be mentioned.

3. The closing paragraph again adds a thanks and states that you look forward to hearing from the interviewer.

It might seem unnecessary to send a thank you letter so quickly after the interview, but doing so will reinforce in the interviewer's mind just how serious and enthusiastic you are about the position. And that very act can separate you from the other applicants, giving you the extra something that leads to your being hired.

ASHLEY K. FLORA

Current Address
909 Sierra Madre Street
Westwood Village, CA 90024
(213) 320-8670

Permanent Address
Cachuma Avenue
Ventura, CA 93004
(805) 649-2367

DEAR PERSONNEL COORDINATOR:

I am interested in applying for the position of Flight Attendent and understand that your airline is currently hiring employees for this position.

I recently graduated with a Bachelor of Arts degree in Communication Studies. My eagerness in pursing a career as a flight attendent will be executed with the utmost enthusiasm, due to your exceptional structure and quality of your training program. I financed my education with experience in public relations and I am confident I would be an asset to your staff. I am outgoing, people oriented, communicate well with others and take pride in being the best. I believe that giving the best service to our passengers is the key to a successful career as a Flight Attendent.

Enclosed is a completed application along with my resume which provides additional information about my experience and education. I may be reached at the addresses and phone numbers above. I will be glad to make myself available for an interview at your convenience to discuss how my qualifications would be consistent with your needs. Thank you so much for your time and consideration.

Sincerely,

Ashley K. Flora

Enclosure: application
           resume
           self-addressed, stamped envelope

CYNTHIA A. CHASE

Current Address
1900 Barry Street
Westwood Village, CA   90024
(213) 320-0458

Permanent Address
234 Periwinkle Drive
Ventura, CA   93004
(805) 644-6782

DEAR PERSONNEL COORDINATOR:

I am interested in applying for an administrative assistant/marketing position at your corporate headquarters. I would like to express a sincere interest in finding out more about becoming an integral part of your staff. I am willing to relocate, as I am aware of your excellent reputation and aggressive commitment to the travel industry.

I will be graduating from the University of California at Los Angeles with a Bachelor of Arts degree in Communication Studies in December 1988. I have gained valuable experience while working and attending college to earn my degree. I am confident I will make a significant contribution to your staff now, and an increasingly important one in years to come. What makes me different from other applicants?

- I have developed strong communication and organizational skills as President/VP of a sorority, earning the "Outstanding Senior Award."
- I am self-motivated, dependable, outgoing and a quick learner.
- Strength in identifying company needs, problems and solutions.
- Special talent for establishing excellent rapport with clients, vendors and fellow employees.
- Demonstrate poise and confidence while speaking in front of large and small groups of all levels of management and personnel.
- An eager desire to learn and the willingness and determination to do what it takes to get the job done.

Enclosed is a completed application along with my resume which provides additional information about my experience and education. I may be reached at the addresses and phone numbers above. I will be glad to make myself available for an interview at your convenience to discuss how my qualifications would be consistent with your needs. Thank you so much for your time and consideration.

Sincerely,

Cynthia A. Chase

Enclosure: application
          resume

DENISE A. LITTLE

Current Address
4999 College Road
Goleta, CA 93117
(805) 222-0800

Permanent Address
1111 Marina Avenue
Concord, CA 94333
(222) 888-8888

PERSONNEL DIRECTOR:

I'm seeking an entry level position leading to an accounting career with your firm. Being aware of your excellent reputation and aggressive commitment to the industry, I would like to express a sincere interest to be a part of your accounting staff.

I will be graduating from the University of California at Berkeley in June 1989. While financing my education with experience in accounting and customer relations, I continue to maintain an accounting GPA of 3.8. Being enthusiastic and dependable with a strong desire to learn and excel, I am confident I will make a significant contribution to your staff now, and an increasingly important one in years to come.

Enclosed is my resume which provides additional information about my experience and education. I may be reached at the addresses and phone numbers above. I will be glad to make myself available for an interview at any time at your convenience to discuss how my qualifications would be consistent with your needs. Thank you for your time and consideration.

Sincerely,

Denise A. Little

Enclosure: Resume

HAYLEY BLAKE
1111 VALLEY ROAD
BOSTON, MA 99999
(206) 555-3390

DEAR PERSONNEL DIRECTOR:

I am interested in applying for an administrative assistant position.

I recently graduated from business college and gained valuable knowledge in computerized office procedures. Being enthusiastic and loyal with the ability to learn quickly and a strong desire to excel, I am confident I will make a significant contribution to your staff. Listed below is a brief qualification summary:

- four years professional experience with clerical office support, phones skills, bookkeeping and management.
- excellent rapport with customers and fellow employees.
- strong organizational skills with attention to detail.
- typing speed 60+ wpm; entry-level word processing skills.

Enclosed is my resume which provides additional information about my experience and education. I will be glad to make myself available for an interview at your convenience to discuss how my qualifications would be consistent with your needs. Thank you for your time and consideration.

Sincerely,

Hayley Blake

Enclosure: resume

HOLLY L. BLAKE

Current Address
111 Camarillo #1
Goleta, CA 93117
(805) 362-8899

Permanent Address
2215 Oak Street
San Francisco, CA 94361
(415) 888-1177

DEAR PERSONNEL DIRECTOR:

I am applying for an elementary teaching position with your school district for the 1989 summer program. My friend, Cynthia Cornellia, a teacher at Magdelana School in San Francisco referred me to you for this position.

I recently passed the CBEST and plan to attend San Francisco State University in the Fall of 1989. My dedication and enthusiasm for teaching extends far beyond the classroom. I enjoy working with parents to help improve their children's education and I feel that involving the community in our educational system is important. I am confident I will make an excellent role model for your students and an important contribution to your staff.

Enclosed is my resume which provides additional information about my education and experience. I may be reached at the addresses and phone numbers above. I will be glad to make myself available for an interview at your earliest convenience to discuss how my qualifications would be consistent with your needs. Thank you for your time and consideration.

Sincerely,

Holly L. Blake

Enclosures

BRIAN B. MATTHEWS
118 Franciso Avenue
Ventura, CA 93003
(805) 966-7281

PERSONNEL DIRECTOR:

I am seeking an entry level position as a Professional Geologist, as my wife and I will be relocating to the greater Seattle area in July, 1988. In the event that your company is recruiting a qualified employee with these skills, please consider me a candidate.

I will be graduating from the University of California at Los Angeles in June 1988 with a Bachelor of Science degree in Geological Sciences. Given my education, proven initiative and success while financing my education, I am confident I will make an important contribution to your staff now, and an increasingly important one in years to come.

Enclosed is my resume which provides additional information about my experience and education. I may be reached at the address and phone number above. I will be glad to make myself available for an interview at your earliest convenience to discuss how my qualifications would be consistent with your needs. Thank you for your time and consideration.

Sincerely,

Brian Matthews

Enclosure: Resume

PAUL BLACK
999 College Avenue
Santa Barbara, CA 93105
(805) 555-1111

PERSONNEL DIRECTOR:

I'm seeking a position leading to a challenging career with your firm. I would like to express a sincere interest in finding out more about becoming a an integral part of your accounting staff.

I graduated from the University of California at Los Angeles in June 1989 and financed my education with experience in accounting. I am confident I will make a signficant contribution to your staff now, and an increasingly important one in years to come.

Enclosed is my resume which provides additional information about my experience and education. I may be reached at the address and phone above. I will be glad to make myself available for an interview at any time at your convenience to discuss how my qualifications would be consistent with your needs. Thank you for your time and consideration.

Sincerely,

Paul Black

Enclosure: Resume

CHRISTOPHER B. FRANCIS

Current Address
22 Churchill Drive
Santa Barbara, CA   93110
(805) 555-1111

Permanent Address
225 Westwood Drive
Los Angeles, CA   90043
(213) 555-2345

PERSONNEL DIRECTOR:

I am interested in applying for the Student Affairs Officer.

As a recent graduate from University of California at Los Angeles, I received my BA degree in Law and Society. What makes me different from other applicants?

- Being a transfer student from a community college to a 4-year university, I offer first-hand experience to provide individual advice to prospective students in the field and in the office.
- I am highly organized, dedicated with a positive attitude.
- Special talent for assessing people's needs and priorities.
- Outstanding ability to communicate with all types of people.
- Work well under pressure situations while maintaining a highly professional and concerned manner.
- Familiar with UC admission requirements.

Enclosed is my application and resume which provides additional information about my experience and education. I may be reached at the addresses and phone numbers above. I will be glad to make myself available for an interview at your convenience to discuss how my qualifications would be consistent with your needs.

Sincerely,

Christopher B. Francis

Enclosure: resume

DENISE L. LANDON
333 Austin Street
Santa Barbara, CA 93111
(805) 222-5678

PERSONNEL COORDINATOR:

I am interested in applying for a part-time position with a reputable law firm. Currently earning my JD degree from the Los Angeles College of Law, I will be graduating in December 1989.

I have developed strong skills in legal writing and research through volunteer work and school projects. With my educational background, proven success in office and project management and desire to learn and excel, I am confident I will make a significant contribution to your staff.

Enclosed is my resume which provides additional information about my education and experience. I may be reached at the address and phone number above. I will be glad to make myself available for an interview at your earliest convenience to discuss how my qualifications would be consistent with your needs. Thank you for your time and consideration.

Sincerely,

Denise L. Landon

Enclosure: Resume

SUSAN M. ALLEN
125126 Avenue
Bellingham, WA 22220
(202) 777-1234

PERSONNEL DIRECTOR:

I am writing in response to our conversation on Friday, December 16, 1988 for the position of Sales Representative. Martin Kramer suggested I contact you. As I am aware of your excellent reputation and aggressive commitment to the industry, I would like to express my <u>sincere</u> interest to be a part of your sales team.

I offer over five years successful experience emphasizing strong sales techniques, exceptional presentation, closing skills and effective customer relations, resulting in production and profitability in highly competitive markets. I am confident I will make an important contribution to your company now, and an increasingly important one in years to come.

Enclosed is my resume which provides additional information about my education and experience. I would appreciate the opportunity to meet with you to discuss how my qualifications would be consistent with your needs.

Sincerely,

Susan M. Allen

Enclosure: Resume

THOMAS W. FRANCHESCA

Current Address:		**Permanent Address:**

Current Address:
100 Freedom Court
Santa Barbara, CA   93101
(805) 666-2345

Permanent Address:
123 Los Sierra Drive
San Diego, CA   94444
(619) 222-7999

DEAR PERSONNEL COORDINATOR:

I am a recent graduate seeking a Paralegal position with your law firm.

I recently received a BA degree in Law and Society from the University of California in Santa Barbara. Currently, I am working for the Commissioner in small claims court in Santa Barbara. In addition, I have worked as an intern at the Own Recognizance Unit as a felony investigator. Along with my experience and educational background, I offer a strong desire to learn and excel and am confident I will make a significant contribution to your staff now, and an increasingly important one in years to come.

Enclosed is my resume which provides additional information about my education and experience. I may be reached at the addresses and phone numbers above. I will be glad to make myself available for an interview at any time at your earliest convenience to discuss how my qualifications would be consistent with your needs. Thank you for your time and consideration.

Sincerely,

Thomas W.   Franchesca

Enclosure: Resume

THOMAS W. FRANCHESCA

<u>Current Address:</u>
100 Freedom Court
Santa Barbara, CA   93101
(805) 666-2345

<u>Permanent Address:</u>
123 Los Sierra Drive
San Diego, CA   94444
(619) 222-7999

March 7, 1989

Ms. Joan Johnson
Keller & Reid
234 Bush, Suite 100
Los Angeles, CA   92222

Dear Ms. Johnson:

I'm writing to let you know how pleased I am with your candor and to thank you for the opportunity to speak with a legal assistant along with the chief, Mr. Perlman.

After spending the majority of my time working on a part-time basis for the municipal court and the Own Recognizance Unit, I am eager to start working full time. I thrive on working in a fast-paced and competitive environment and can assure you I am ready for intense work and will work hard until the job is finished and completed correctly.

To reiterate, I'd like to let you know that I am impressed with Keller and Reid and would like to express my sincere interest to be part of your legal staff. I look forward to hearing from you in the following weeks. Thank you so much for your time and consideration.

Sincerely,

Thomas W. Franchesca

July 5, 1989

John Gregory
Assistant Vice President
Bellingham Savings & Loan
3333 State Street
Bellingham, WA 22299

Dear Mr. Gregory:

Thank you for the opportunity of interviewing me for the position of Personnel Clerk today. Being aware of your excellent reputation and aggressive commitment to the banking industry, I would be proud to be a member of your team.

I would like to express a <u>sincere</u> interest to be a part of your personnel staff. I am confident I will make an important contribution to you and your customers now, and an increasingly important one in years to come.

Sincerely,

Franchesca Antoine

Chapter VII
JOB SEARCHING & INTERVIEWING

Proven Successful Job Search Techniques

What is the best way to find a job? Follow the steps below:

1. Look in the Yellow Pages directory under the type of company or industry that interests you.

2. Bypass the personnel department as their function is to screen out potential employees, a negative screen process.

3. Directly contact the manager in charge of the (accounting, research, etc.) department. Why? Because you may have skills related or indirectly related to the profession you're interested in that only the department manager would be aware of after talking to you. (I've learned this to be true in many cases through my own experiences.)

    a. Bypassing personnel can be tricky! A good receptionist will screen your call and direct you to the appropriate department. For your call that means PERSONNEL.

    b. Unfortunately, if the receptionist asks who you are and why you are calling, it may be essential that you provide another reason why you need to speak with the manager.

4. When you do get through, ask if there are any positions available and tell him/her that your resume is in the mail; send a cover letter and resume to him/her directly.

5. Wait three days and telephone your contact again. Ask if your resume was received; set up an appointment for an interview.

Many jobs are not advertised. The manager you talk to will be impressed that you thought to bypass personnel. It works quite effectively. Remember to always check your local paper's classified ads, especially the Sunday issue to see who and what is being advertising. You may find a position available that interests you.

Another great place to look for jobs is in trade journals at your local school or public library. Large and medium-sized corporations as well as smaller companies will advertise in trade journals for employees from all over the country for professions such as law, biology, journalism or teaching. Even the fashion industry has a trade journal with an employment section. Most professions have a trade journal magazine or news- letter. Ask your librarian for the name of the trade journal or newsletter that would cover your profession or field of interest.

> **FOR EXAMPLE:** If you would like to work for a daily or weekly news- paper, as reporter, editor, manager, graphic artist or advertising representative, *Editor & Publisher* is the trade journal for the newspaper industry. You'll find many jobs listed from entry-level to high level executive positions in the classified section at the back of the magazine.

About Jobs With GPA Requirements

Many management trainee programs with major department store chains require recent graduates to have at least a 2.9 or 3.0 Grade Point Average (GPA). Contact your Career Counseling Center to find out the GPA requirements of any employers offering on- campus interviews. It is true that some major corporations such as Price Waterhouse and the Associated Press take only students from the cream of the crop. That is to say, students with a GPA of 3.5 or above. The key word here is <u>students</u>. Once you've proven yourself on the job at another company or corporation for three years, you're not considered a recent graduate and are no longer even asked for your transcripts. REMEMBER, those of you who haven't quite made a 3.5 GPA need not worry. Your GPA only follows you around for your first three years after graduation, <u>not</u> for the rest of your life. What should you do about it? Plan on gaining your first three years of experience with one of those companies that does not have the high GPA requirement. If a company has a 3.5 or above GPA requirement, they usually say so when they advertise. If you're not responding to an advertisement, ask anyone in the Personnel Department; they should know.

You will find many good companies out there without such a requirement. After gaining work experience, three years after graduation, apply for a position at the corporation you originally desired. Believe me, if you follow this rule of thumb, you will eliminate a lot of wasted time and headaches in your search for employment.

About Student Part-Time Employment

Most of you soon-to-be graduates are seeking full-time work. But what if you're a first- or second-year student seeking part-time employment in your field of study? Go for it! The key word here is part-time employment. To some employers, a first-year student means stability. Employers feel there's a good chance students will plan on staying with the company throughout their school years. That could mean 2-4 years of employment for you.

How to Apply For a Job With the Airlines

Each airline receives over 500 applications a month. Because of this competition, it is absolutely necessary to follow each airline's specific up-to-date rules when applying for employment. Simply telephone information and ask for the specified airline's employment number. (Sometimes they will have an 800 number.)

When you call, in many cases, you will hear a recording of employment opportunities along with the proper procedure to apply. Some airlines require you to first send a self-addressed, stamped envelope with a letter requesting an application. Then you'll mail a completed application, resume and cover letter. Some airlines even require you to send a check for $10 just to process your application. The airlines are very competitive and service-oriented. The key to getting an interview is to focus your resume and application on service, service and more service. They want to know what you can do for them, not what they can do for you.

Scenario: An Interview For a Banking Position

Sometimes, though, you can express what a job will do for you and still have it sound like a benefit for the company. While interviewing for a banking position many years ago, I was asked, "How did you feel about your first banking job?" I thought about that very first job, a file clerk in the trust department of a bank - not a very exciting position. But I responded, "I was 18 years old and felt good about being a file clerk at the bank because working for a bank is stable. I had job security." They were pleased with my response, which stressed the positive, and I did get hired.

Looking for job security is actually something most employers like to hear. It confirms in their minds that you really are planning to stay with the company for awhile. Even if you're looking for a short-term internship, it won't hurt to say you're looking for an internship leading to a career opportunity with the company.

Helpful Hints: Things to Know Before the Interview

Interviewing is an art in itself. Here are some helpful hints to think about before going on the interview.

1. Call your local Chamber of Commerce and ask for information about the company. In the interview, when they ask if you know about the company, it is very impressive to demonstrate that you did some research before you came in.

2. For out-of-town companies, check with the reference librarian of your library for more information about the firm.

3. Bring 3 or 4 resumes with you on the interview. You could be interviewed

by 1-3 employers. Hand a resume to each interviewer and always keep one for yourself. Chances are the interviewer will use your resume to interview you, and this will make the interview go a lot smoother for both of you. It's okay to refer to your resume during the interview, though I suggest you try to memorize the main points of the resume beforehand.

4. Always bring a pad of paper and pen to the interview. Ask questions about the job and take notes. You may want to jot down a few questions before you go on the interview. Also, remember to write the interviewer's name and title (with the correct spelling) on your note pad to address a thank you letter after the interview.

5. Remember, think positive! Focus on your strengths. Talk about what you do have to offer, not what you don't. If you're applying for a position you do not have experience in, focus on enthusiasm and eagerness to learn. Do not to even think about the fact that you don't have experience. Enthusiasm is a great asset that employers notice. Sometimes the employer would rather train an enthusiastic employee with no experience than hire an experienced employee without it.

6. After the interview, immediately send a thank you letter to the potential employer.

List of References & Letters of Recommendation

Most employers will ask for three personal and/or business references. A "reference" is simply the listing of names, professional title, company they work for, company address and phone number of those who will give you a reference. Always let your contacts know prior to using their name as a reference that you plan to do so and make sure they will give you a GOOD one. It's usually unnecessary to mail references with your resume and cover letter unless requested. It is, however, a good idea to bring them with you to the interview along with a letter of recommendation. A letter of recommendation is the letter written by a previous employer on the company stationery, highly recommending you for the position. If it doesn't, don't use it.

What to Wear on the Interview

Always dress up for an interview. Your appearance will be the interviewers' first impression of you. WOMEN should wear a nice dress or skirt and blouse. For on-campus interviews it is highly recommended that women wear a nice blazer suit jacket to compliment a mid-length skirt and blouse in conservative colors. This could be modified, of course, if you are auditioning for a singer in a rock band.

MEN should dress conservatively in a suit; YES, that means slacks, nice shirt, jacket and tie. Even if you know the company employees wear jeans on the job, you are not an employee, yet. You want to look businesslike and professional. Dressing up for the interview shows the employer you take your work seriously. Believe me, it will make a difference.

ORDER INFORMATION

TANGERINE PRESS
1315 Whedbee Street
Ft. Collins, CO 80524
(303) 224-5065/FAX 224-4778

Please send me the following books by Kim Marino:

_____ *The College Student's Resume Guide (2nd Edition)* **$9.95**
ISBN# 0-9624284-7-7

_____ *The Resume Guide For Women of the '90s* **$11.95**
ISBN# 0-9624284-8-5

_____ *Starting a Successful Resume Writing Service* **$49.95**

Name: . . . .
. . . .
Address: . . . .
. . . .
. . . .

Shipping:$3.00 for the first book and 50 cents for each additional book.